"This series is a tremendous resource for those ... understanding of how the gospel is woven th... pastors and scholars doing gospel business fro... logical feast preparing God's people to apply the entire Bible to all of the w... wholly committed to Christ's priorities."

BRYAN CHAPELL, President Emeritus, Covenant Theological Seminary; Senior Pastor, Grace Presbyterian Church, Peoria, Illinois

"Mark Twain may have smiled when he wrote to a friend, 'I didn't have time to write you a short letter, so I wrote you a long letter.' But the truth of Twain's remark remains serious and universal, because well-reasoned, compact writing requires extra time and extra hard work. And this is what we have in the Crossway Bible study series *Knowing the Bible*. The skilled authors and notable editors provide the contours of each book of the Bible as well as the grand theological themes that bind them together as one Book. Here, in a 12-week format, are carefully wrought studies that will ignite the mind and the heart."

R. KENT HUGHES, Visiting Professor of Practical Theology, Westminster Theological Seminary

"*Knowing the Bible* brings together a gifted team of Bible teachers to produce a high-quality series of study guides. The coordinated focus of these materials is unique: biblical content, provocative questions, systematic theology, practical application, and the gospel story of God's grace presented all the way through Scripture."

PHILIP G. RYKEN, President, Wheaton College

"These *Knowing the Bible* volumes provide a significant and very welcome variation on the general run of inductive Bible studies. This series provides substantial instruction, as well as teaching through the very questions that are asked. *Knowing the Bible* then goes even further by showing how any given text links with the gospel, the whole Bible, and the formation of theology. I heartily endorse this orientation of individual books to the whole Bible and the gospel, and I applaud the demonstration that sound theology was not something invented later by Christians, but is right there in the pages of Scripture."

GRAEME L. GOLDSWORTHY, former lecturer, Moore Theological College; author, *According to Plan*, *Gospel and Kingdom*, *The Gospel in Revelation*, and *Gospel and Wisdom*

"What a gift to earnest, Bible-loving, Bible-searching believers! The organization and structure of the Bible study format presented through the *Knowing the Bible* series is so well conceived. Students of the Word are led to understand the content of passages through perceptive, guided questions, and they are given rich insights and application all along the way in the brief but illuminating sections that conclude each study. What potential growth in depth and breadth of understanding these studies offer! One can only pray that vast numbers of believers will discover more of God and the beauty of his Word through these rich studies."

BRUCE A. WARE, Professor of Christian Theology, The Southern Baptist Theological Seminary

KNOWING THE BIBLE

J. I. Packer, Theological Editor
Dane C. Ortlund, Series Editor
Lane T. Dennis, Executive Editor

* * * * * *

Genesis	Psalms	Jonah, Micah, and Nahum	Ephesians
Exodus	Proverbs		Philippians
Leviticus	Ecclesiastes	Haggai, Zechariah, and Malachi	Colossians and Philemon
Numbers	Song of Solomon		
Deuteronomy	Isaiah	Matthew	1–2 Thessalonians
Joshua	Jeremiah	Mark	1–2 Timothy and Titus
Judges	Lamentations, Habakkuk, and Zephaniah	Luke	
Ruth and Esther		John	Hebrews
1–2 Samuel	Ezekiel	Acts	James
1–2 Kings	Daniel	Romans	1–2 Peter and Jude
1–2 Chronicles	Hosea	1 Corinthians	1–3 John
Ezra and Nehemiah	Joel, Amos, and Obadiah	2 Corinthians	Revelation
Job		Galatians	

* * * * * *

J. I. PACKER was the former Board of Governors' Professor of Theology at Regent College (Vancouver, BC). Dr. Packer earned his DPhil at the University of Oxford. He is known and loved worldwide as the author of the best-selling book *Knowing God*, as well as many other titles on theology and the Christian life. He served as the General Editor of the ESV Bible and as the Theological Editor for the *ESV Study Bible*.

LANE T. DENNIS is CEO of Crossway, a not-for-profit publishing ministry. Dr. Dennis earned his PhD from Northwestern University. He is Chair of the ESV Bible Translation Oversight Committee and Executive Editor of the *ESV Study Bible*.

DANE C. ORTLUND (PhD, Wheaton College) serves as senior pastor of Naperville Presbyterian Church in Naperville, Illinois. He is an editor for the Knowing the Bible series and the Short Studies in Biblical Theology series, and is the author of several books, including *Gentle and Lowly: The Heart of Christ for Sinners and Sufferers*.

EZRA AND NEHEMIAH

A 12-WEEK STUDY

Kathleen B. Nielson

:: CROSSWAY®

WHEATON, ILLINOIS

Crossway is a publishing ministry of Good News Publishers.

VP		31	30	29	28	27	26	25	24
16	15	14	13	12	11	10	9	8	7	6

TABLE OF CONTENTS

SERIES PREFACE

KNOWING THE BIBLE, as the series title indicates, was created to help readers know and understand the meaning, the message, and the God of the Bible. Each volume in the series consists of 12 units that progressively take the reader through a clear, concise study of that book of the Bible. In this way, any given volume can fruitfully be used in a 12-week format either in group study, such as in a church-based context, or in individual study. Of course, these 12 studies could be completed in fewer or more than 12 weeks, as convenient, depending on the context in which they are used.

Each study unit gives an overview of the text at hand before digging into it with a series of questions for reflection or discussion. The unit then concludes by highlighting the gospel of grace in each passage ("Gospel Glimpses"), identifying whole-Bible themes that occur in the passage ("Whole-Bible Connections"), and pinpointing Christian doctrines that are affirmed in the passage ("Theological Soundings").

The final component to each unit is a section for reflecting on personal and practical implications from the passage at hand. The layout provides space for recording responses to the questions proposed, and we think readers need to do this to get the full benefit of the exercise. The series also includes definitions of key words. These definitions are indicated by a note number in the text and are found at the end of each chapter.

Lastly, for help in understanding the Bible in this deeper way, we would urge the reader to use the ESV Bible and the *ESV Study Bible*, which are available online at esv.org. The *Knowing the Bible* series is also available online.

May the Lord greatly bless your study as you seek to know him through knowing his Word.

J. I. Packer
Lane T. Dennis

WEEK 1: OVERVIEW OF EZRA AND NEHEMIAH

Getting Acquainted

Ezra and Nehemiah were, for centuries, received as one book narrating the return of God's exiled[1] people to their land, as under Persian rule they were allowed to resettle and rebuild Jerusalem. These two books cover three different waves of returning exiles, from 538 to 433 BC. But they tell one story: the restoration of God's covenant[2] people according to his Word—which they are now called afresh to obey.

This restoration required, first of all, the rebuilding of the temple and the reinstitution of ceremonial worship. The first leader, Zerubbabel, led the initial wave of exiles back to Jerusalem to accomplish this goal (Ezra 1–6). The second wave came more than half a century later, led by Ezra, who rebuilt not the temple but the people, teaching them—and calling them to obey—the law of Moses (Ezra 7–10).

Thirteen years after Ezra arrived, Nehemiah returned to Jerusalem. He first led the people to rebuild the wall (Nehemiah 1–6). Then, along with Ezra, he sought to restore the people (Nehemiah 7–13) as God's holy nation, followers of his Word.

The restoration was not complete, however. These books picture God's people regathered but struggling—they are poor subjects of a foreign king; their city is devastated; enemies oppress from without; sin threatens from within. We see the faithful hand of God mercifully preserving his people according to his promises. We also see the dire need for the perfect fulfillment of God's promises in the salvation accomplished by his Son. (For further background, see the *ESV Study Bible*, pages 799–803 and 821–823; available online at esv.org.)

Placing Ezra and Nehemiah in the Larger Story

Ezra and Nehemiah give the last glimpse of Old Testament history. It is a desolate glimpse in many ways. This people is the "offspring" (literally "seed") of Abraham, blessed as God promised, growing into a great nation (Gen. 12:1–7), but then punished for their rebellion through enemies who defeated them and took them into exile. These books show God's unfailing promises to bless this people, restored to their land and the privilege of worshiping God in his temple. But they are a weak remnant, serving the Persian king, with no sign of the promised eternal king on the throne of David (see 2 Sam. 7:12–17). These books cause us to peer forward to the coming of that King, that Deliverer who would bring blessing through this people to all the nations of the world.

Key Passage

"O LORD God of heaven, the great and awesome God who keeps covenant and steadfast love with those who love him and keep his commandments, let your ear be attentive and your eyes open, to hear the prayer of your servant that I now pray before you day and night for the people of Israel your servants." (Neh. 1:5–6)

Date and Historical Background

Because of his people's unfaithfulness, God had allowed the northern kingdom to be conquered by the Assyrians (722 BC), and the southern kingdom of Judah to be conquered by the Babylonians (586 BC). Both defeats involved exile to foreign lands. When King Cyrus of Persia overthrew the Babylonians, he issued a decree (538 BC) allowing the exiled Jews to return to their land. Ezra and Nehemiah shine a light into the postexilic years, telling of three main returns and three central leaders: Zerubbabel (538 BC), Ezra (458 BC), and Nehemiah (445 BC).

Both Ezra and Nehemiah contain first-person narratives; the stories in Nehemiah are especially substantial and vivid. The author(s) of the remaining sections are unknown. The two books were probably finished soon after the events of Nehemiah, approximately 430 BC.

Outline

Ezra

   I. Cyrus's Decree and the *First* Return of Exiles from Babylon (1:1–2:70)

   II. The Returned Exiles Rebuild the *Temple* on Its Original Site (3:1–6:22)

   III. Ezra the Priest Leads the *Second* Return to Rebuild the *People* by Teaching the Law of Moses (7:1–8:36)

   IV. Ezra Discovers and Confronts the Problem of Intermarriage (9:1–10:44)

Nehemiah

   I. Nehemiah Leads the *Third* Return to Jerusalem to Rebuild Its *Walls* (1:1–2:20)

   II. The Wall Is Rebuilt, Despite Difficulties (3:1–7:4)

   III. A Record of Those Who Returned from Exile (7:5–73)

   IV. The *People* Are Rebuilt around God's Word, Leading to Covenant Renewal (8:1–10:39)

   V. Results of Covenant Renewal (11:1–12:47)

   VI. Nehemiah Deals with Problems in the Community (13:1–31)

As You Get Started

Read the first chapter of Ezra and the first two chapters of Nehemiah. What common words and themes emerge?

Read through each book without stopping. What stands out? What questions do you have at the start of this study?

We will learn from some great examples of leadership in these books. But for what reasons will it be important to focus on God's perfect ways, not simply on Ezra's or Nehemiah's pretty good ones?

What are some of your specific hopes and prayers for this study of Ezra and Nehemiah?

As You Finish This Unit . . .

Take a few minutes to ask God to bless you with increased understanding and a transformed heart and life through your study of Ezra and Nehemiah.

Definitions

[1] **Exile** – Several relocations of large groups of Israelites/Jews have occurred throughout history, but "the exile" typically refers to the Babylonian exile, that is, Nebuchadnezzar's relocation of residents of the southern kingdom of Judah to Babylon in 586 BC (residents of the northern kingdom of Israel had been resettled by Assyria in 722 BC).

[2] **Covenant** – A binding agreement between two parties, typically involving a formal statement of their relationship, a list of stipulations and obligations for both parties, a list of witnesses to the agreement, and a list of curses for unfaithfulness and blessings for faithfulness to the agreement. Throughout Old Testament times, God established covenants with his people, all of which he faithfully keeps, and all of whose benefits climax in Christ, who inaugurates the new covenant in his blood (1 Cor. 11:25).

Week 2: The First Return—by God's Stirring

Ezra 1–2

The Place of the Passage

The Place of the Passage

These first chapters set the narrative in its historical context and establish the main action: King Cyrus releases God's people from exile to return home to Jerusalem and Judah. But these chapters also establish the larger narrative perspective: this is the story of God being faithful to his Word and acting on behalf of his people (see Ezra 1:1).

The Big Picture

Ezra 1–2 tells of King Cyrus's decree that the people of Judah be released from exile to return and rebuild God's house in Jerusalem. Gifts and provisions are given, and stolen treasures from the Jerusalem temple are restored—all to be carried home by those listed in a detailed census.

Reflection and Discussion

Read Ezra 1–2, praying for insight as you begin and observing carefully as you go. Then write your reflections on the following questions. (For further background, see the *ESV Study Bible*, pages 804–807; available online at esv.org.)

1. The Proclamation of King Cyrus (1:1–4)

First, let's set this story in context. Turn one page back and read 2 Chronicles 36. Make several observations about how the conclusion of Chronicles connects to the opening of Ezra.

Read Jeremiah 25:11–14 (Jeremiah prophesied during Judah's fall to the Babylonians). Read also Isaiah 44:24–45:7 (Isaiah foresaw these events a century in advance). What truths about God do these verses reveal?

King Cyrus sent numerous groups of exiles back to their various countries in order to curry the favor of as many local gods as possible. He calls God what the Jews called him: "the LORD, the God of heaven." What ironies are here in 1:1–4? Compare and contrast the Persian king's perspective with God's perspective.

2. Getting It All Together (1:5–11)

Consider the words about God's stirring up people's spirits (Ezra 1:1, 5). Why are these glimpses into the activity of God so important here? What difference do these glimpses make to you today?

Find the references to the "house of the LORD" in Ezra 1 and then read about the dedication of the temple in 1 Kings 7:51–8:11 (skim the rest of 1 Kings 8). Briefly sum up what the temple represented for God's people.

Why is such attention given to these treasures in Ezra 1:4–11? (Read Ex. 12:35–36 and comment on parallels here.)

3. The People (2:1–70)

Read chapter 2. What do you notice? Why are these lists wonderful and crucial at this point in salvation history?

Read in Numbers 3:1–20 about God's choosing the Levites to care for temple worship, with only Aaron's line serving as priests.[1] In what ways does Ezra 2 highlight the importance of the temple and its workers?

The leaders listed first are Zerubbabel and Jeshua (v. 2). Read more about them in Haggai 1, and write a few brief observations.

Read through the following three sections on *Gospel Glimpses*, *Whole-Bible Connections*, and *Theological Soundings*. Then take time to consider the *Personal Implications* these sections may have for you.

Gospel Glimpses

RELEASE FROM CAPTIVITY. The Bible reveals a God who delivers a captive people. The exodus[2] of God's people from Egypt is the great Old Testament story of deliverance, retold by generations. The release from exile repeats the story of deliverance from captivity; Ezra 2:1 rings with the solemn import of it. Isaiah long before had connected Cyrus with God's "anointed"[3] who would save his people (Isa. 45:1). When Jesus the promised Christ appeared, he accomplished what was foreshadowed in the exodus and the release from exile: deliverance from the slavery of sin and death, through his death on sinners' behalf and his resurrection from the dead. Praise God for his Son, who came to "proclaim liberty to the captives" (Isa. 61:1; Luke 4:16–21; John 8:34–36; Rom. 8:1–2).

A PEOPLE FOR HIMSELF. Ezra shows God's hand on the precious remnant of God's called-out people, through whom he is working his redemptive plan (Ezra 1:3; 2:1).[4] Ezra highlights these "survivor[s]" (1:4; see Isa. 10:20–22), and his enumeration of them shows God's faithful preservation through the dispersion of the exile. From the time of his promise concerning Eve's seed (Gen. 3:15), God has been revealing a plan to redeem a people for himself through his Son. This plan was at work in his covenant with Abraham, that from him would come a great nation, blessed by God and a blessing to the nations. The Bible traces this covenant people from Abraham's descendants, through the generations of those from whom the promised seed would come, through the line of David, to Jesus himself. In our time, Abraham's descendants—not by bloodline but by faith in the blood of Christ—join the redeemed people who are God's treasured possession (Gal. 3:7–9; 1 Pet. 2:9–10). The Bible tells of a called-out people, and the postexilic glimpse of the restored remnant of this people is a crucial episode in the salvation story.

Whole-Bible Connections

A STORY ABOUT GOD'S WORD. "Whole-Bible Connections" are at the heart of Ezra's message! His opening point is that Cyrus's decree fulfilled God's word (Ezra 1:1). But it's not just that specific prophecies were fulfilled. These books offer the final Old Testament link in the whole flow of redemptive history—set in motion by God's spoken word at creation, ordained by God's word to Eve, and channeled by God's words of promise from Abraham all the way to the Word-made-flesh. Ezra's account emerges in the bright background light of God's unfailing word that has called out and preserved this people according to his promises. Amid the grim reality of rebuilding a broken-down city as slaves to a foreign king, the surety of God's word supplies a foundation of faith in God and hope for the final fulfillment of all his promises.

THE TEMPLE. This book's focus on the temple is established immediately, reminding us of the Lord's eternal purpose to dwell with his people. After the expulsion of Adam and Eve from the garden of Eden because of their sin, the rest of Scripture tells of making a way for a holy God to dwell with an unholy people. God told Moses to have the people build a tabernacle "that I may dwell in their midst" (Ex. 25:8). The priesthood and sacrificial system were God's merciful provision to allow a sinful people to approach him. The Jerusalem temple offers the climactic Old Testament picture of God's presence with his people, with his glory filling it upon its dedication (1 Kings 8:10–11). After the exile, then, rebuilding this "house of the LORD" (1:3) is central for the regathered people of God. But the glory is gone—only to reappear in the One who came to tabernacle with us and show us God's glory in the flesh (John 1:14).

The New Testament shows Jesus himself to be the true temple (John 2:18–21), embodied in his people through his Spirit (Eph. 2:19–22), and ultimately shining among them in the heavenly Jerusalem (Rev. 21:3, 22).

RICHES FROM THE NATIONS. The temple vessels that had been carried off from Jerusalem were now restored to God's people (Ezra 1:7–11), as Jeremiah had prophesied (Jer. 27:21–22). But there's more: by Cyrus's decree, rich gifts of silver and gold and cattle and supplies were given by the Persians as parting assistance to the Jews (Ezra 1:4, 6). How can we not find echoes here of Exodus 3:21–22, where God promises Moses that his released people would "plunder the Egyptians" as they leave? (See Ex. 11:2–3; 12:35–36; 36:2–7.) Scripture consistently shows that God owns the nations and all their goods—and will in fact have all of it for himself and his people in the end. Into the new Jerusalem will be brought the "glory and the honor of the nations" (Rev. 21:24–26; see also Isa. 60:10–14).

Theological Soundings

SOVEREIGNTY OF GOD.[5] Along with showing the consequential actions of all the people in this story, Ezra reveals a sovereign God who directs all the action. We have seen God's unfailing word revealed though his prophets. Ezra pulls back the curtain even further to reveal God "stirring up the spirit" of Cyrus to make his proclamation and stirring up the spirit of the Jews to rebuild the house of God (Ezra 1:1, 5). This book reveals a God who directs the course of history and the hearts of kings, which are like streams of water in the Lord's hand (Prov. 21:1). Ezra helps us grasp the Lord's sovereign power in relation to every human event—the same sovereign power God declared in advance to Cyrus through the prophet Isaiah (Isa. 45:4–7).

WORSHIP DUE GOD. God's faithful preservation of his people according to his word calls for a personal response of worship—coming into his presence with praise, ascribing to God the honor due his name. The focus on the temple shows God's merciful provision of a place and a ceremonial system whereby his people could approach him in worship, as indeed his people must do. To such a sovereign, righteous, and merciful God is due all worship and praise. All the gold and silver and plunder of these chapters offers just a hint of the riches due the King of heaven, who created and owns it all. Ezra 2 closes with the faithful remnant returning to Jerusalem and offering freewill offerings for the house of God (vv. 68–69). We glimpse here a response to an eternal call to worship, worship that now pours out to the risen Christ, worship ultimately described in Revelation 15:4: "All nations will come and worship you, for your righteous acts have been revealed."

Personal Implications

Take time to reflect on the implications of Ezra 1–2 for your own life today. Consider what you have learned that might lead you to praise God, repent of sin, and trust in his gracious promises. Make notes below on the personal implications for your walk with the Lord of the (1) *Gospel Glimpses*, (2) *Whole-Bible Connections*, (3) *Theological Soundings*, and (4) this passage as a whole.

1. Gospel Glimpses

2. Whole-Bible Connections

3. Theological Soundings

4. Ezra 1–2

> ### As You Finish This Unit . . .

Take a moment now to ask for the Lord's blessing and help as you continue in this study. Take a moment also to look back through this unit, to reflect on some key things that the Lord may be teaching you—and perhaps to highlight and underline these things to review again in the future.

Definitions

[1] **Priest** – In OT Israel, the priest represented the people before God, and God before the people. Although the whole tribe of Levites was given duties overseeing worship, only those descended from Aaron could be priests. Priests' prescribed duties also included inspecting and receiving sacrifices from the people and overseeing the daily activities and maintenance of the tabernacle or temple.

[2] **Exodus** – The departure of the people of Israel from Egypt and their journey to Mount Sinai under Moses' leadership (Exodus 1–19; Numbers 33). The exodus demonstrated God's power and providence for his people who had been enslaved by the Egyptians. The annual festival of Passover commemorates God's final plague upon the Egyptians that resulted in Israel's release from Egypt.

[3] **Anoint** – In Scripture, to pour oil (usually olive oil) on someone or something to set the person or thing apart for a special role in God's service. Anointing was performed for the high priest, for tabernacle vessels, for kings, and for prophets. The Hebrew word *Messiah* and its Greek equivalent *Christ* both mean "anointed one."

[4] **Redemption** – In the context of the Bible, the act of buying back someone who had become enslaved or something that had been lost to someone else. Through his death and resurrection, Jesus purchased redemption for all believers (Col. 1:13–14).

[5] **Sovereignty** – Supreme and independent power and authority. Sovereignty over all things is a distinctive attribute of God (1 Tim. 6:15–16). He directs all things to carry out his purposes (Rom. 8:28–29).

WEEK 3: TEMPLE REBUILDING— AND OPPOSITION

Ezra 3–4

▲

The Place of the Passage

With their journey completed, the returned exiles focus immediately on the Jerusalem temple in chapters 3–4. The first task of rebuilding the altar and the foundation (ch. 3) shows the obedient worship and ensuing rejoicing of God's people. The challenge from adversaries (ch. 4) shows the nature and methods of those who oppose the Lord and his people—often with temporary success.

The Big Picture

These chapters show the priority of worship among God's people as they celebrate his steadfast love from generation to generation. Yet, at this point of rejoicing, both the weeping of the elders and the opposition of enemies remind us that God's redemptive plan is not yet complete.

> ## Reflection and Discussion

Read Ezra 3–4. Then write your reflections on the following questions that take us into these initial scenes of exiles returned to the land of promise. (For further background, see the *ESV Study Bible*, pages 807–810; available online at esv.org.)

1. Rebuilding the Altar (3:1–7)

Briefly comment on the phrases in verses 1–7 that reveal the guide and the motivation for the people's activity.

An altar was for sacrifices offered to God—all kinds of sacrifices, on ordinary days and feast days. Read in Exodus 29:38–46 about the daily sacrifices; in Leviticus 16:29–34 about special instructions for the seventh month; and in Leviticus 23:33–43 about the Feast of Booths. Why was the altar (and, by implication, the ceremonial system of worship) so important for the Israelites?

According to Hebrews 10:1–14, why don't believers today need a physical altar? According to Hebrews 10:15–25 and 13:9–15, what kind of an altar do we have?

2. Rebuilding the Temple Foundation (3:8–13)

Picture the sights and sounds of the joyful scene as God's people worship and celebrate the temple foundation! Look back to King David's song as he led God's people in worship (1 Chron. 16:4–36, especially v. 34). What is the consistent focus as God's people worship? Consider the way David's words grow richer in meaning generation by generation—even to our day.

What can we discern from the text about the reasons for the people's weeping (Ezra 3:12–13)? How might 1 Kings 8:1–11 help?

Think of our worship celebrations today as followers of the risen Christ. Compare and contrast the ways in which we rejoice—and yet still weep. How can this Old Testament scene encourage and exhort us as New Testament believers?

3. Repeated Opposition (4:1–24)

First, let's clarify the chronology, which includes two jumps forward—a common literary device—to show that opposition from enemies continued to occur:

- Ezra 4:1–5 describes opposition to the first group of returned exiles under Zerubbabel (beginning 538 BC, during the reign of Cyrus).

- Ezra 4:6 jumps forward to oppression during the reign of Ahasuerus (or Xerxes I, king 486–464 BC—when Esther lived).
- Ezra 4:7–23 jumps forward again to oppression during the reign of Artaxerxes I (464–423 BC—which was during the time of Ezra and Nehemiah).
- Ezra 4:24 picks up the story again from 4:5, moving back to the time of Zerubbabel but also moving forward from the reign of Cyrus to a later king, Darius (whose second year would have been 520 BC, making the period of inactivity under Zerubbabel about 15 years).

It is good to be aware of the methods commonly employed by adversaries to halt God's people and God's work. What various methods of adversaries can you observe in this chapter? Which have you observed or experienced personally?

According to Ezra 3–4, in what various ways did the people deal with the adversaries surrounding them "Beyond the River" (the name given by the Persians to the province that included Judah and Jerusalem)? Write your observations and comments.

Jump forward to the time of Jesus and read his words to his disciples in John 15:18–20. Jump forward again to read the apostle Paul's words in Ephesians 6:10–13. What do these words tell us about facing opposition as Christians today?

Read through the following sections on *Gospel Glimpses, Whole-Bible Connections,* and *Theological Soundings*. Then take time to consider the *Personal Implications* these sections may have for you.

Gospel Glimpses

THE ALTAR. God's instructions concerning an altar of sacrifice reveal his merciful provision of a way for his sinful people to approach him. Without the mediation of priests and sacrifices, an unholy people could never live as the special people of a holy God. Only "when Christ had offered for all time a single sacrifice for sins" was, finally, an altar of blood sacrifice no longer needed. Until that time, the altar stood central to the lives of God's people, reminding them of his holy presence and gracious provision. Just as God provided for Abraham a ram to offer on his altar in place of his son Isaac (Gen. 22:9–14), so God in the fullness of time sent his own Son as the "Lamb of God, who takes away the sin of the world" (John 1:29).

GOD'S STEADFAST LOVE. As they celebrate, God's people sing their praises and thanksgiving responsively: "He is good, for his steadfast love endures forever toward Israel" (Ezra 3:11). They are praising the unchanging character of the God of their salvation. Their song, echoing the words sung in anticipation of Solomon's temple (1 Chron. 16:34), highlights the same "steadfast love" God declared to Moses (Ex. 34:6; Deut. 7:9) and that rings out repeatedly in the Psalms (see, for example, Ps. 32:10; 33:18–22). This "steadfast love" is the covenant love of God, his unfailing kindness toward his people, shown ultimately in the sending of his Son for their salvation. The steadfast love of the Lord endures forever—in Christ, the risen, eternal Lord.

Whole-Bible Connections

SACRIFICES. An altar of blood sacrifice was no longer needed after Christ's death and resurrection, but the Bible does not stop talking about priests or sacrifices! Belonging to Christ, who gave himself for us as the perfect sacrifice, we are called now to be a "holy priesthood, to offer spiritual sacrifices acceptable to God though Jesus Christ" (1 Pet. 2:5). Through him we "continually offer up a sacrifice of praise to God, that is, the fruit of lips that acknowledge his name" (Heb. 13:15). Only through God's mercies to us in Christ can we now present our bodies as a "living sacrifice, holy and acceptable to God"— which is not our physical worship on an altar, but our "spiritual worship" in Christ (Rom. 12:1).

OPPOSITION TO GOD'S PEOPLE. With its layer upon layer of opposition, this story offers a vivid example of how God's people in all times and in various ways live out the tensions Jesus talked about in John 15:18–19—being chosen out of the world and hated by the world. The Old Testament reality of physical struggle helps us grasp the spiritual battle Paul describes, not "against flesh and blood, but against the rulers, against the authorities, against the cosmic powers over this present darkness, against the spiritual forces of evil in the heavenly places" (Eph. 6:12). This is the battle Christ first fought and won for us (Col. 2:13–15) so that we could by his Spirit put on the "armor of God" and "stand firm" (Eph. 6:12–13). Ever since Eden, believers are participating in the ongoing story of rebellion against God; the rebels were defeated at the cross, and at the last day the Lord Jesus will put all his enemies under his feet (1 Cor. 15:25–28).

Theological Soundings

GOD'S PEOPLE IN GOD'S PRESENCE. The scene of rejoicing in Ezra 3 gives a small glimpse of what God's people lost in Eden and what is restored to God's people in Christ: the joy of living in his presence as his people. The loud, elaborate celebration, simply for a completed foundation, offers just a faint hint of the heavenly celebrations of the redeemed around the throne of the Lamb (Rev. 5:8–14). This scene in Ezra's time is a little like that scene yet to come, because the temple represented God's dwelling with his people. However, to many older observers the new temple seemed inferior to the former temple built by Solomon. Here was no ark of the covenant or shining glory of God's presence—and those who carried those memories wept. Joy lights up this scene because of God's steadfast love, but the weeping reminds us that the full manifestation of that love had not yet been given.

KINGSHIP. Ezra 4 is full of kings' names! It is helpful to see not only that each king ruled over God's people, but also that each of these kings passed away, giving place to the next—while God's people are continually preserved, even as he promised. An earthly king's decree is powerful for a time, and yet this book began with the great Persian King Cyrus acting according to the word of the Lord, who is the God of heaven and every nation on earth. "I am God, and there is no other," declares the Lord in Isaiah 45 (vv. 5, 6, 18, 22), the chapter in which Cyrus's actions are foretold. The prophet Isaiah's (and the whole Bible's) perspective is shaped by the vision of the Lord "sitting upon a throne, high and lifted up" (6:1), sovereign above earth's temporary sovereigns. The wonder of the Bible's story is that this King of Heaven came down to us—the eternal King promised in the line of King David (2 Sam. 7:12–13; Ps. 132:11–12), the King who came to die, but who is now the resurrected King who "must reign until he has put all his enemies under his feet" (1 Cor. 15:26).

> **Personal Implications**

Take time to reflect on the implications of Ezra 3–4 for your own life today. Consider what you have learned that might lead you to praise God, repent of sin, and trust in his gracious promises. Make notes below on the personal implications for your walk with the Lord of the (1) *Gospel Glimpses*, (2) *Whole-Bible Connections*, (3) *Theological Soundings*, and (4) this passage as a whole.

1. Gospel Glimpses

2. Whole-Bible Connections

3. Theological Soundings

4. Ezra 3–4

As You Finish This Unit . . .

Take a moment now to ask for the Lord's blessing and help as you continue in this study. And take a moment also to look back through this unit, to reflect on key things that the Lord may be teaching you—and perhaps to highlight and underline these things to review again in the future.

WEEK 4:
REBUILDING AGAIN—
AND RESOLUTION

Ezra 5–6

▲

The Place of the Passage

Chapter 4 ended with the temple rebuilding stopped, and for a time the adversaries seemed to have won. Chapters 5–6 show God's sovereign hand in the resumption and completion of the work—culminating in a joyful dedication of the rebuilt temple and the celebration of ceremonial practices there. These passages complete the book's first half, resolving the story of the first group of returned exiles under Zerubbabel.

The Big Picture

These chapters make clear that God is overseeing the reestablishment of this remnant according to his word and for his redemptive purposes. The centrality of the temple emphasizes his merciful provision of a way for his chosen people to come into his presence and worship him.

Reflection and Discussion

Read Ezra 5–6. Then write your reflections on the following questions. (For further background, see the *ESV Study Bible*, pages 810–814; available online at esv.org.)

1. God's Word, God's Leaders, and God's Eye (5:1–5)

How beautiful to see what God did to urge his people back to the task of rebuilding! Read Ezra 5:1–2, and for background read Haggai 1 and Zechariah 1:1–17; 4:1–10. What can we learn here about God and his ways?

Consider the three-pronged leadership God provides his people at this time: prophets, a priest in the line of Aaron, and a ruler (Zerubbabel) in the line of King David. (On Zerubbabel, see the *ESV Study Bible* note on Hag. 1:1.) In what ways do these leaders together picture the one perfect leader still to come?

Read Ezra 5:1–5 and Psalm 33:13–19. Comment on the perspective given by these verses—and the importance of this perspective for God's people both then and now.

2. Working It Out with King Darius (5:6–6:12)

First, we have a copy of the letter sent by local officials to Darius, asking whether this rebuilding project had been sanctioned by King Cyrus. Read this letter (Ezra 5:6–17) and jot down words and phrases that stand out. Notice especially the words used to name God and his people. (Note: "Sheshbazzar" is perhaps another name for Zerubbabel or the name of an earlier governor.)

The letter inspires King Darius to search for records of Cyrus's decree (recall 1:1–4). Read the results (6:1–12) and list the requirements of Darius's decree. What strikes you? What was King Darius evidently seeking? And what was God clearly doing for his people?

Darius refers to the "God who has caused his name to dwell there"—this "house of God that is in Jerusalem" (v. 12). In what ways does Darius get God's purposes exactly right? See Deuteronomy 12:1–11 and 1 Kings 8:27–30.

3. Resolution and Celebration (6:13–22)

What layers of authority work to bring about the resolution reported in Ezra 6:13–15? What is the effect of these summary verses?

Compare Ezra 6:16–18 with 1 Kings 8:62–66 to find ways in which the dedication of the rebuilt temple recalls the dedication of the first one under King Solomon. What do the various parts of this ceremony in Ezra 6:16–18 in effect declare before God?

Finally, they celebrate the Feast of Passover (vv. 19–22). What do you notice about those who participate? What did the Passover commemorate, and how is this especially meaningful at this time (see Ex. 12:1–20)?

In what ways does the final verse of this section (Ezra 6:22) bring an appropriate conclusion and focus? (Recall the initial focus in 1:1.)

Read through the following sections on *Gospel Glimpses, Whole-Bible Connections,* and *Theological Soundings.* Then take time to consider the *Personal Implications* these sections may have for you.

Gospel Glimpses

ACKNOWLEDGMENT OF SIN. God's people are clearly aware that this destruction and exile came about because of their own sin. God has been merciful to redeem them. They tell their history honestly: "Because our fathers had angered the God of heaven, he gave them into the hand of Nebuchadnezzar king of Babylon" (Ezra 5:11–12). Chapter 6 carefully points out the "sin offering" on behalf of "all Israel"—with no exceptions. The sin is pervasive. This is a people whom God did not choose for their righteousness, but he set his steadfast love on them and provided for them the means to deal with their sin—namely, the sacrificial system they are working obediently to reinstitute. Ultimately he provided full and final purification from sin through their seed—Jesus, who knew no sin but was made sin for us, "so that in him we might become the righteousness of God" (2 Cor. 5:21).

PASSOVER. The celebration of Passover concludes this section, recalling God's deliverance of his people from slavery in Egypt, and the Passover lamb without blemish, whose blood on the doorpost and lintel of a house delivered those inside from death. As these returned exiles "slaughtered the Passover lamb" (Ezra 6:20), they praised the God who rescued his people from slavery in Egypt and now from exile in Babylon. They praised the God who delivers his people—ultimately from sin and death through Christ's blood shed for us on the cross. The far-reaching scope of this deliverance is hinted at in this scene, as the Passover meal is eaten by the returned exiles and "also by every one who had joined them and separated himself from the uncleanness of the peoples of the land to worship the LORD, the God of Israel" (6:21). The joy permeating this scene is the joy of salvation that will spread through this people to all the nations of the earth.

Whole-Bible Connections

PROPHETS. The appearance of Haggai and Zechariah offers a wonderful whole-Bible connector, as we link this story with the prophets who brought God's word to the characters in the story. The prophetic books come alive in our understanding when we set them in their historical contexts—some (like Isaiah) bring God's word in advance of the exile; some (like Jeremiah) speak directly into the exile; and a few (like Haggai and Zechariah) prophesy to the returned remnant. God sends his word into every part of the history of his people. Just as the "prophets of God were with them, supporting them" (Ezra 5:2), so God in every age provides his people with his living and active Word, now given us in the completed inspired Scriptures. How instructive to see God overseeing this remnant both by stirring the hearts of kings from afar and by bringing his word right to his people, a needed "support." The greatest support would ultimately come through the Word made flesh—Jesus the Messiah, who is God with us fully and finally.

CALENDARS AND PROPHECIES. In Old Testament narratives the Jewish calendar is consistently in view, with the various feast days marking seasons and events. We read that the temple rebuilding was "finished on the third day of the month of Adar, in the sixth year of the reign of Darius the king" (Ezra 6:15). Not only does such specificity root these stories in history, it also provides context for ceremonial practices. Adar (our February/March) was the last month of the Jewish year, and the next month (the "first month"; v. 19) brings the celebration of Passover. In God's providence the people complete and dedicate the temple just in time to begin the whole cycle of feast days, starting with the crucial Passover celebration. These carefully recorded dates also reveal that about 70 years have passed between the destruction of the first temple (586 BC) and Darius's sixth year (515 BC). This period of time offers one way to understand the fulfillment of Jeremiah's prophecy of a 70-year exile (Jer. 25:11–12; 29:10).

▶ Theological Soundings

GOD'S SOVEREIGN SHAPING OF HISTORY. This section emphasizes God's sovereign shaping of events; it is an account of God at work on behalf of his people. He sends the prophets with his strengthening word (Ezra 5:1–2; 6:14). "The eye of their God" protects the Jewish elders (5:5). The rebuilding happens by his decree (6:14), and the actions of earthly kings occur as he determines them (6:22). It is he who makes his people joyful (6:22)! Along with the local focus on the temple comes a larger focus on God's sovereign hand over all nations and all of history. As the apostle Paul preached, "The God who made the world and everything in it, being Lord of heaven and earth, does not live in temples made by man. . . . He made from one man every nation of mankind to live on all the face of the earth, having determined allotted periods and the boundaries of their dwelling place" (Acts 17:24–26).

GOD'S NAME. King Darius might not understand, but he rightly says that God "caused his name to dwell" in his "house" (Ezra 6:12). Names in the Scriptures often represent a person's essence—hence name changes such as Abram to Abraham or Jacob to Israel. By designating the temple as the place where he would "put his name and make his habitation" (Deut. 12:5), God was deigning to reveal his glorious self to his people in that place—even though that place could not hold his transcendent being. The wonder of the Bible's story is the wonder of God's revealing his name to us—as he did to Moses with the words "I AM WHO I AM" (Ex. 3:14). But the greatest wonder is the revelation of himself in his Son, who has been given the "name that is above every name, so that at the name of Jesus every knee should bow"—not just in a temple but "in heaven and on earth and under the earth" (Phil. 2:9–11).

Personal Implications

Take time to reflect on the implications of Ezra 5–6 for your own life today. Consider what you have learned that might lead you to praise God, repent of sin, and trust in his gracious promises. Make notes below on the personal implications for your walk with the Lord of the (1) *Gospel Glimpses*, (2) *Whole-Bible Connections*, (3) *Theological Soundings*, and (4) this passage as a whole.

1. Gospel Glimpses

2. Whole-Bible Connections

3. Theological Soundings

4. Ezra 5–6

As You Finish This Unit . . .

Take a moment now to ask for the Lord's blessing and help as you continue in this study. And take a moment also to look back through this unit, to reflect on some key things that the Lord may be teaching you—and perhaps to highlight and underline these things to review again in the future.

WEEK 5: A SECOND RETURN—BY GOD'S GOOD HAND

Ezra 7–8

▲

The Place of the Passage

After the temple is rebuilt, the book moves forward 57 years to focus on a second returning group, led by Ezra. There's a new Persian king (Artaxerxes), and there is the same pattern of God's sovereign direction of the king to bless and prosper the returning remnant. Chapters 7–8 mirror the process of preparation we saw in Ezra 1–2. Here it is Ezra who is sent by the king, this time not to rebuild but to teach the "laws of your God" (7:25–26).

The Big Picture

Ezra 7–8 initiates a second wave of God's sovereign blessing on the returning exiles, this time not through physical rebuilding but through spiritual rebuilding according to his Word.

Reflection and Discussion

Read Ezra 7–8. Then write your reflections on the following questions. (For further background, see the *ESV Study Bible*, pages 814–817; available online at esv.org.)

1. Getting to Know Ezra the Scribe (7:1–10)

First, write a short character study of Ezra from these verses, highlighting the most important things about this man.

If you were going to use Ezra 7:10 as a text for a devotional, what might be your outline?

We cannot focus merely on Ezra. Find the references to God in verses 1–10. What crucial perspective do these references provide?

2. Ezra and the King (7:11–28)

More letters! With multiple lists and letters, these postexilic narratives document the history of the hand of God on his people. Read 7:11–26, and then look back to chapter 1. What similar themes do you find, and how are they developed even more richly in this scene decades later? What does the king send Ezra to do, and what can you discern about the king's motives (ch. 7)?

How does Ezra respond to such abundant provision (7:27–28)? These verses begin a section of personal memoir from Ezra. What words stand out, and why?

Read Isaiah 41:8–10 and Psalm 106:40–48—the kinds of passages Ezra must have known and cherished. What words stand out, and why?

3. The Return (8:1–36)

Ezra 8:1–14 closely parallels the list in chapter 2, with many common family names; clans are converging in this second return. This group pauses by a river (v. 15) and discovers there are no sons of Levi among them—no "ministers for the house of our God" (8:17). By what various means is this issue addressed (vv. 15–20)? What wisdom can we heed from this passage?

What further principles of godly wisdom emerge in 8:21–23? We'll see Nehemiah reach a different conclusion about accepting military protection (Neh. 2:7–9). Even amid diverse strategic decisions, what heart attitudes and core principles must remain the same?

Ezra 8:24–34 describes an exercise in faith. What kinds of faith were required here, amid what sorts of tests? What various hands help shape this story? What can we learn from reading it?

Upon arriving in Jerusalem, what various activities does this group of returned exiles engage in (vv. 35–36), and how do these activities provide a perfect ending for this whole section of the story?

Read through the following sections on *Gospel Glimpses, Whole-Bible Connections,* and *Theological Soundings*. Then take time to consider the *Personal Implications* these sections may have for you.

Gospel Glimpses

THE LORD WHO CALLS US TO SEEK HIM. Ezra's words of witness to the king ring out: "The hand of our God is for good on all who seek him" (8:22). This section bears witness to a God who hears the prayers of those who humbly seek him—as Ezra and the people do there by the river for three days, fasting, "that we might humble ourselves before our God, to seek from him a safe journey" (8:21). They "implored" God, and he "listened to [their] entreaty" (8:23). The premise of the law that Ezra teaches is that God therein reveals himself to us, that we might respond by seeking and knowing him. The Bible's call is to "seek the LORD while he may be found; call upon him while he is near" (Isa. 55:6). God has come near to us and has fully revealed himself to us in his Son, who came to seek us, die for us, rise again, and bid us follow him in faith. Truly, the hand of our God is for good on all who seek him, through faith in the Lord Jesus Christ.

WRATH OF GOD. Ezra's words of witness to the king continue: "the power of his wrath is against all who forsake him" (8:22). Ezra was not afraid to declare that God responds with grace to those who seek him but with wrath against those who refuse. The gospel is good news because it tells how God delivers sinful rebels from the wrath they deserve (Eph. 2:3). Even unbelieving kings have a sense of guilt and sin that deserves divine wrath: Artaxerxes pours out gifts for this "God of heaven" who lives in Jerusalem, "lest his wrath be against the realm of the king and his sons" (7:23). Artaxerxes does not know that God cannot be bought but must be humbly sought. Deliverance from God's wrath comes by grace to those who seek him according to his Word and through the Savior revealed in it (Rom. 5:8–9).

Whole-Bible Connections

LEADERS IN ISRAEL. From the beginning God called out leaders: patriarchs like Abraham, prophets, priests, judges, heads of tribes and families, eventually kings. The kingdom fell because of corrupt leaders who rejected God's word. Ezekiel, for example, prophesied against the "shepherds of Israel" who fed themselves and did not feed the sheep (Ezek. 34:1–6). That background lights up Ezra's story, as he gathers "leading men from Israel" (Ezra 7:28) and addresses the lack of Levitical leaders (8:15). We notice a strong cluster of "leading men" and a couple "men of insight" whom Ezra can send to the "leading man" at Casiphia (8:15–17). When it comes time to carry the treasure, the responsibility is given to "twelve of the leading priests" (8:24). Part of God's gracious hand on this remnant clearly involved the raising up of faithful leaders among them. Today we pray for God's continued raising up of faithful leaders in families and churches, and for those leaders to be good shepherds of the flock as they serve and follow the "chief Shepherd," the Lord Jesus (1 Pet. 5:1–4).

MORE WEALTH OF THE NATIONS. We can't miss the "over-the-top" flow of provision here (Ezra 7:12–26). Ezra is to take not just silver and gold freely offered by king and counselors, but "all the silver and gold that you shall find in the whole province of Babylonia" (7:15–16). After a list of generous provisions (including unlimited supplies of salt!), Ezra also receives direct access to the king's treasury (7:20). Ezra responds with an outburst of praise not to Artaxerxes but to the Lord, "who put such a thing as this into the heart of the king, to beautify the house of the Lord"—directly quoting from a prophecy of Isaiah looking forward to the "wealth of the nations" coming to God's people (Isa. 60:1–14). Ezra sees all this abundance as an extension of God's "steadfast love" (Ezra 7:28), evidence of God's providential hand as Ezra moves forward in obedience to his heavenly king. He is faithfully participating in a grand story of redemption that will culminate around a heavenly throne, with the treasures of nations laid at the feet of the risen Christ.

▶ Theological Soundings

THE LAW OF MOSES. In these chapters the law of Moses receives prominent mention, as Ezra is a scribe "skilled" in that law.[1] We learn first that this law comes from God: it is the "Law of Moses that the Lord, the God of Israel, had given" (Ezra 7:6). We learn that by this law God means to transform hearts and lives: Ezra had set his heart to study it, do it, and teach it in Israel. King Artaxerxes repeatedly mentions the law and Ezra's expertise in it, grasping its importance as a connection to Israel's God—and its condemnation of those who do not obey it (7:26). What King Artaxerxes does not grasp is the law's merciful revelation of God's redemptive plan at work through God's chosen people. As chapter 8 closes with the returned exiles offering burnt offerings and sin offerings to God, as prescribed by the law, we glimpse the amazing grace and mercy of this Word from God that opens a way for people to come to him and live.

HUMAN RESPONSIBILITY AND DIVINE SOVEREIGNTY. In this book we encounter the eye of God and the hand of God—his *sovereignty*. We're watching God directing the course of history in order to accomplish his redemptive purposes. Ezra, an outstanding individual leader, offers a vivid example of wise human leadership—which must take its place alongside, but not in competition with, the sovereign hand of God that is shaping this story. Ezra worked hard and became skilled in the law—and the good hand of his God was on him (7:6, 9–10). Ezra masterfully handled the need for more Levites—and the good hand of God was on them (8:18). Ezra conceived a wise plan to transport the treasures—and the hand of God protected them (8:31). From the start we see the larger perspective: every part of this story happens according to God's unfailing word. Through wise characters like Ezra (and Nehemiah), we begin to grasp the beautiful response of obedience to a sovereign God—obedience acted out perfectly only within the Godhead, by the Son to the Father, according to God's redemptive plan established before the foundation of the world (Eph. 1:3–4).

Personal Implications

Reflect on the implications of Ezra 7–8 for your own life today. Consider what you have learned that might lead you to praise God, repent of sin, and trust in his gracious promises. Make notes below on the personal implications for your walk with the Lord of the (1) *Gospel Glimpses*, (2) *Whole-Bible Connections*, (3) *Theological Soundings*, and (4) this passage as a whole.

1. Gospel Glimpses

2. Whole-Bible Connections

3. Theological Soundings

4. Ezra 7–8

▶ As You Finish This Unit . . .

Take a moment now to ask for the Lord's blessing and help as you continue in this study. And take a moment also to look back through this unit, to reflect on some key things that the Lord may be teaching you—and perhaps to highlight and underline these things to review again in the future.

Definition

[1] **Law** – When spelled with an initial capital letter, "Law" refers to the first five books of the Bible (the Pentateuch), written mainly by Moses. The Law contains the earliest history of God's dealings with his people, including numerous commands of God, including the Ten Commandments and instructions regarding worship, sacrifice, and life in Israel.

Week 6: People Rebuilding— and Confession

Ezra 9–10

▲

The book concludes with dark seriousness. The law Ezra teaches convicts the people of their disobedience through intermarriage with women from neighboring unbelieving peoples. We see the unworthiness of this people and, even more, the holiness of this God at whose word we must tremble, and the mercy of this God who covenants with sinners for saving purposes.

The Big Picture

Ezra leads his people in repentance before the Lord for their disobedience to his laws concerning intermarriage with surrounding nations. Not only repentance, but sorrowful reparation as well, ends this glimpse into the reestablished remnant of God's people.

Reflection and Discussion

Read Ezra 9–10, prayerfully taking in the sober conclusion to this book. Then write your reflections on the following questions. (For further background, see the *ESV Study Bible*, pages 817–820; available online at esv.org.)

1. Ezra Prays (9:1–15)

Read Deuteronomy 7:1–11. What parts of that passage help us understand the nature of the sin revealed in Ezra 9:1–2? What parts of Ezra 9:1–2 highlight the grievous nature of the sin?

"Holy race" (v. 2) means literally "holy seed or offspring." In order to be clear that the Bible is not talking about anything like racism or discrimination based on ethnicity, look back to Ezra 6:21. How does that verse show the welcome available to any foreign convert? (Recall Rahab and Ruth; see also Ex. 12:38 and the "mixed multitude.") Further, read Genesis 12:1–7 and 15:1–6. What is to be accomplished through the preservation of this holy seed?

Consider the response in Ezra 9:3–5. What strong words and actions stand out? What does it mean to tremble at the words of the Lord (see also 10:3 and

Isa. 66:1–2)? In what ways do we take God's Word this seriously as his people today? In what ways do we not do so?

Now read Ezra's moving prayer (Ezra 9:6–15) and briefly comment on repeated words and key words. How would you sum up what Ezra is saying about God's people and about God?

2. Repenting and Putting Away (10:1–44)

In what specific ways might the response in 10:1–5 inspire both deep hope and honest skepticism? Now read verse 6; how does it add to your reflections?

Read Ezra 10:7–15, in which the people respond to the call to *separate themselves* (10:11). This episode is difficult, partly because we do not know what happened to these women and children who were "put away" (10:3, 19). They were likely sent back to their own peoples. We know these women had not "separated [themselves] from the uncleanness of the peoples of the land to worship the LORD," as had the foreigners welcomed into the worshiping community of God's people (6:21). From this covenant community context we cannot draw implications for today about individual Christians divorcing unbelieving spouses; indeed, the apostle Paul specifically commands otherwise (1 Cor. 7:12–14). Certainly we must draw implications about whom we as believers choose to marry. The larger parallels relate to keeping ourselves "unstained from the world" (James 1:27). The "abominations" from which God's people had not separated themselves included, above all, idolatry—worshiping false gods and participating in associated evil practices. These things had led to the people's exile (Ezra 9:1, 11, 14; see also 2 Chron. 36:14). Here is the question for us: How do 2 Corinthians 6:14–7:1 and Ephesians 5:1–14 similarly call God's people to separate themselves?

The people's sin is a deadly serious matter, and the process of dealing with it is hard and long. What words and details in this final chapter accentuate this truth?

Finally, step back and wonder again at God's sovereign plan to put Ezra in this place at this time. He couldn't fix these people, but what *could* he do? Did he?

Read through the following sections on *Gospel Glimpses*, *Whole-Bible Connections*, and *Theological Soundings*. Then take time to consider the *Personal Implications* these sections may have for you.

Gospel Glimpses

GUILT AND GRIEF OF SIN. Ezra responds with intensity to the people's sin (9:3). His prayers grapple with the grief of sin against a holy God who has been so merciful—yet who is "just" and punishes sin with his "wrath" (9:15; 10:14). "Iniquities," "guilt," and "faithlessness" echo through the narrative, pounding home the truth of sin like the pelting rain in the last scene. Even though Ezra is not personally complicit in this sin, he uses the first person plural and identifies with his people, making us think of Christ, the great High Priest who personally identified with our sin, died for it, and purifies us from it.

GOD'S FAVOR. For Ezra, the guilt of sin emerges even more clearly in light of God's merciful favor to this remnant. The "brief moment" of favor is God's bringing them back to the Promised Land and enabling them under a foreign king to rebuild the temple, granting them a "secure hold within his holy place, that our God may brighten our eyes and grant us a little reviving in our slavery" (v. 8). What a beautiful picture of God's mercifully bringing them home and opening the way for them to come into his presence as his chosen people. God has punished them less than their iniquities deserved (9:13). Through Jesus Christ, all believers are indeed punished less than our iniquities deserve; we are given not just a brief moment of favor but an eternity.

Whole-Bible Connections

UNCLEANNESS. Ezra grieves that God's people have not obeyed him by separating themselves from the uncleanness of surrounding nations—the uncleanness of sinful souls. The needed cleansing, although not ultimately physical, is pictured physically in the Scriptures—hence the purification rituals, circumcision, and the restrictions on food and people who are "unclean" through disease, blood flow, and so forth (see Leviticus 11–15). This theme comes to fruition in the ministry of Jesus, who comes to heal all kinds of uncleanness—including ultimately the uncleanness of sin separating human beings from God. When the leper in Mark 1:40 says, "If you will, you can make me clean," his words ring with the truth of salvation. Truly, by God's mercy and through the blood of Jesus comes the "washing of regeneration" that cleanses our souls from sin (Titus 3:5).

PRAYER AND FASTING. In these chapters, Ezra turns directly to God. His immediate impulse is to prostrate himself before the Lord in fasting and prayer—because he knows the Lord who hears his prayer. He loves the Lord and is grieved to the core by sin against him. What an example for us—

prayer and fasting coming from the heart, and trembling at God's Word. Throughout the Scriptures come warnings against the kind of prayer and fasting that have become mere rituals or "for show"; God delights in those who seek him with all their hearts (Joel 2:12–13). Jesus taught his disciples to pray and fast as those communing humbly with our Father in heaven (Matt. 6:5–18). And Jesus himself opened the way for every believer to draw near with confidence, in full assurance of faith, with hearts sprinkled clean (Heb. 10:19–23).

> ## Theological Soundings

HOLY SEED. This "holy race" or "seed" (Ezra 9:2) grows and makes a pathway throughout the Scriptures, leading to Christ alone. After Adam and Eve sinned, God decreed that the "offspring" ("seed") of the woman would one day bruise the head of the Serpent (Gen. 3:15). God promised Abraham that his "offspring"/"seed" would be great, blessed by God and bringing blessing to all the nations, dwelling in the land of promise (Gen. 12:1–7; 15:1–6). In Galatians, the apostle Paul carefully explains that when these promises were made to Abraham, they referred to his "offspring" in the singular, "referring to one, 'And to your offspring,' who is Christ" (Gal. 3:16). The wonder for us today is that, as Paul explains, "If you are Christ's, then you are Abraham's offspring, heirs according to promise" (Gal. 3:29).

COVENANTS. God's covenants with his people require their obedience but depend on God's faithfulness. In Ezra's last chapters, the people have "broken faith" (Ezra 9:2; 10:2, 10) with their God—they have broken his covenant with them. When they cry, "Let us make a covenant with our God to put away all these wives," we rejoice in their renewed will to obey, but we also wince, knowing they will not and cannot perfectly keep the covenant they have just made—as we will see in the book of Nehemiah. We are reminded here both of God's steadfast love to a people who break faith and of God's faithfulness to his covenant with these people, a covenant to be finally fulfilled only through his Son, Jesus Christ.

> ## Personal Implications

Reflect on the implications of Ezra 9–10 for your own life today. Consider what you have learned that might lead you to praise God, repent of sin, and trust in his gracious promises. Make notes below on the personal implications for your walk with the Lord of the (1) *Gospel Glimpses*, (2) *Whole-Bible Connections*, (3) *Theological Soundings*, and (4) this passage as a whole.

1. Gospel Glimpses

2. Whole-Bible Connections

3. Theological Soundings

4. Ezra 9–10

> ## As You Finish This Unit . . .

Take a moment now to ask for the Lord's blessing and help as you continue in this study. Take a moment also to look back through this unit, to reflect on some key things that the Lord may be teaching you—and perhaps to highlight and underline these things to review again in the future.

WEEK 7: A THIRD RETURN—BY GOD'S GOOD HAND

Nehemiah 1–2

The Place of the Passage

Thirteen years after Ezra led his group back to Jerusalem, Nehemiah returns. And, just as we saw Ezra (and Zerubbabel before him) sent off with the generous blessing of a Persian king, so Nehemiah is granted aid from King Artaxerxes, whom he serves in the court at Susa. As we read Nehemiah's first-person memoir of his return, we are shown again the hand of God in preserving the remnant of his people—and in raising up this godly man to lead them.

The Big Picture

Chapters 1–2 show God's hand on Nehemiah as he weeps for Jerusalem, seeks the Lord in prayer, approaches the king for help, and makes the journey from Susa to Jerusalem to rebuild the broken-down wall.

> ### Reflection and Discussion

Look back through the overview of Ezra–Nehemiah in Week 1. Then read Nehemiah 1–2 and write your reflections on the following questions. (For further background, see the *ESV Study Bible*, pages 824–826; available online at esv.org.)

1. A Report and a Prayer (1:1–11)

In Nehemiah 1:1–3, what familiar key words stand out, establishing the focus of this book? In verses 1–4, what things do we immediately learn about Nehemiah? (Review the background in Ezra 4:7–23.)

From Nehemiah's record in 1:4–11, what might we observe and learn about the prayer of a godly man? Make a list, being sure to include the beauty of prayer based on God's Word (see Deut. 4:25–31; 7:6–11).

How does the first chapter show clearly Nehemiah's view of God and of himself? Why is this an important beginning for this book?

2. Before the King (2:1–8)

After four months of prayer, Nehemiah is ready for the journey to Jerusalem. In this scene before King Artaxerxes, in what specific ways are Nehemiah's thoughtful preparations evident?

How does Nehemiah communicate that the king's favor is due not to Nehemiah's own wisdom or other personal qualities but to the God of heaven?

3. In Jerusalem (2:9–20)

Make some observations about Nehemiah's approach to leadership in his early days in Jerusalem (vv. 11–18). Notice again the contrast in strategy with Ezra— but the similar bent of heart (recall Ezra 8:21–23).

In verses 9–10 and 19–20, what clear insights does Nehemiah give us about the enemies of God's people? Comment on his reply to them (v. 20; see also Ezra 4:1–3).

WEEK 7: A THIRD RETURN—BY GOD'S GOOD HAND

Christians today do not battle as a nation against other peoples. What is the nature of our battle and our weapons, according to 2 Corinthians 10:4–6, Ephesians 6:10–20, and 1 Thessalonians 5:8? How were these postexilic leaders called to wield the same weapons? In what ways do you wield them?

Read through the following sections on *Gospel Glimpses, Whole-Bible Connections,* and *Theological Soundings.* Then consider the *Personal Implications* these sections may have for you.

Gospel Glimpses

REDEMPTION OF A REMNANT. Nehemiah continues Ezra's focus on this remnant of God's people who have survived the exile and whom God delivers safely home to Jerusalem (Neh. 1:2–3). We find here a growing focus on God's redemptive work—delivering his people from slavery in Egypt, the Babylonian exile, and ultimately sin and death through the salvation accomplished in his Son. When Nehemiah prays, "They are your servants and your people, whom you have redeemed by your great power and by your strong hand" (1:10), his words resonate with the truth of God's plan of redemption. Nehemiah's people have been imperfect "servants," exiled because of their sin. To redeem them finally, God will send his perfect servant, who comes "not to be served but to serve, and to give his life as a ransom for many" (Mark 10:45).

INTERCESSION[1] ON BEHALF OF A SINFUL PEOPLE. The book of Ezra ended with Ezra the priest praying and confessing the sin of his people. This book begins with Nehemiah doing the same (Neh. 1:4). Both of these men identify with the people's sin (see 1:6–7), but neither one, priest or not, can bring about cleansing from sin. Both acknowledge God's word that has been broken and God's justice in punishing his people for breaking it. But both throw themselves on God's mercy; Nehemiah closes his prayer by asking for mercy (1:11). These praying men, godly but imperfect, point forward to the need for a perfect intercessor, one who through his death on their behalf and his resurrection from the dead can present his people blameless before the presence of God's glory (Jude 24). Jesus is our great and sufficient intercessor, even now raised and at the right hand of God, interceding for us (Rom. 8:34).

Whole-Bible Connections

JERUSALEM. Even more than Ezra, which focused on Jerusalem's temple, the book of Nehemiah focuses on the city of Jerusalem. For God's people, this city and its temple represented the place chosen by God for his name to dwell (Neh. 1:9). The prophet Isaiah lamented the downfall of Jerusalem, picturing her as an unfaithful "whore" (Isa. 1:21). But he foresaw Jerusalem's redemption: "You shall be called the city of righteousness, the faithful city" (Isa. 1:26–27). With such words Isaiah and other prophets pointed forward not only to promised restoration from exile; they pointed forward ultimately to the "holy city, new Jerusalem, coming down out of heaven from God, prepared as a bride adorned for her husband" (Rev. 21:2). In that city God will dwell forever with his people: "He will dwell with them, and they will be his people, and God himself will be with them as their God" (Rev. 21:3).

PRAYING WITHOUT CEASING. Ezra and Nehemiah make a beautiful link in the Bible's story of human beings' communing with God. Their narratives offer a personal glimpse into the prayer lives of these leaders who tell their own stories and record their own prayers. We learn the importance of sustained, repentant prayer filled with God's Word—confessing in light of it and claiming its promises (see Neh. 1:8–9). Not only do we see formal prayers; we also watch lives into which the habit of prayer is interwoven—as in Nehemiah's quick "bullet prayer" (see 2:4). Paul's instruction to "pray without ceasing" is no new concept (1 Thess. 5:17). The Lord Jesus offered the perfect example of a life lived in spiritual communion with his Father in heaven. Now, through the indwelling Spirit of the risen Christ, every believer is called and able to live a life full of daily, active communion with God.

Theological Soundings

GOD'S PEOPLE AND NOT GOD'S PEOPLE. In Ezra we saw the importance of God's people separating themselves from surrounding nations. The Old Testament repeatedly shows those who are not God's people threatening and attacking those who are. Nehemiah boldly articulates this distinction to his enemies: "You have no portion or right or claim in Jerusalem" (Neh. 2:20). He is asserting a distinction that God himself made and brings about. God alone calls out a people, from Abraham onward. The process involves separation and cleansing (Ezek. 36:24–28). In the Old Testament it involved calling a nation of people, although true cleansing always happened in individual hearts through faith in God's word—hence Rahab could become part of God's people (and see Hosea 2:23). And thus the unfaithful among God's people could forfeit their special privileges. The whole process climaxes in Jesus, the cornerstone who is either accepted or rejected (1 Pet. 2:4–8). The heavenly Jerusalem, where God dwells forever with his people, is presented in contrast to the lake of eternal fire, reserved for those who are not his redeemed people (Rev. 20:11–21:8). From beginning to end the Bible makes a life-and-death distinction between those who are the people of God and those who are not.

THE LORD GOD OF HEAVEN. Ezra opens with the big picture of fulfilled prophecy and God's sovereignty over kings. By contrast, Nehemiah opens in the first person, with a personal perspective. He does refer to God with the title even pagan kings used ("God of heaven"; see Neh. 1:4 and 2:4). But he also addresses God personally, using the covenantal name "LORD," or "Yahweh"[2] (1:5, 11). Nehemiah shows both the sovereign power of our "great and awesome God" and the relational love of the Lord "who keeps covenant and steadfast love with those who love him and keep his commandments" (v. 5). In comparison to Nehemiah's relationship with the Lord as his "servant" (vv. 6, 11), his role as cupbearer to the king is almost incidental. Throughout the book this perspective will be important: God is the sovereign God of heaven, and he is the Lord who personally oversees his people. We new covenant believers worship this same sovereign God, who in the fullness of time sent his own Son to accomplish the promised redemption of his people.

Personal Implications

Reflect on the implications of Nehemiah 1–2 for your own life today. Consider what you have learned that might lead you to praise God, repent of sin, and trust in his gracious promises. Make notes below on the personal implications for your walk with the Lord of the (1) *Gospel Glimpses,* **(2)** *Whole-Bible Connections,* **(3)** *Theological Soundings,* **and (4) this passage as a whole.**

1. Gospel Glimpses

2. Whole-Bible Connections

3. Theological Soundings

4. Nehemiah 1–2

> ## As You Finish This Unit . . .

Take a moment now to ask for the Lord's blessing and help as you continue in this study. Take a moment also to look back through this unit, to reflect on some key things that the Lord may be teaching you—and perhaps to highlight and underline these things to review again in the future.

Definitions

[1] **Intercession** – Appealing to one person on behalf of another. Often used with reference to prayer.

[2] **Yahweh** – The likely English form of the name represented by the letters YHWH, translated from the Hebrew, where it echoes the verb "I AM" (Ex. 3:14). The Lord revealed this unique name for himself to Moses at the burning bush and told him to instruct the Israelites to call on him by this name. English translations of the Bible usually render this term as "LORD," with small capital letters.

Week 8: Wall
Rebuilding—in Spite
of Opposition

Nehemiah 3–6

The Place of the Passage

Once in Jerusalem, Nehemiah leads the work of rebuilding and of trusting God throughout the process. We see the unity of God's people (ch. 3) in spite of external opposition (chs. 4 and 6) and internal strife (ch. 5). Finally the wall is complete, the building accomplished "with the help of our God" (6:16).

The Big Picture

Chapters 3–6 show the process of rebuilding Jerusalem's wall—with Nehemiah's godly leadership, in spite of threats from without and within, and ultimately through faith in the Lord God who helps them.

Read Nehemiah 3–6. Then write your reflections on the following questions. (For further background, see the *ESV Study Bible*, pages 827–835; available online at esv.org.)

1. Working Together despite Opposition (3:1–4:23)

What words and details in chapter 3 emphasize the unity of God's people in this task of rebuilding? How does 1 Corinthians 12:12–31 help us think about the unity of God's people in the present context of the church?

Chapter 4 of Nehemiah is full of opposition and threats. Examine the nature of these threats and note specific details that stand out. Do you recognize, and have you witnessed, such threats against the work of God's people today?

Examine and list the various responses of God's people in chapter 4, especially those of Nehemiah himself. Note the various affirmations about God forming the basis of these responses.

2. Threats from Within (5:1–19)

For background, read Deuteronomy 15:12–15 and 24:10–15. What is the issue in Nehemiah 5:1–13, and how does Deuteronomy shed light on it?

Note the various stages of Nehemiah's response (vv. 1–13). Which do you find most thought-provoking or convicting, and why?

Note the ways Nehemiah offers himself as an example (vv. 14–19). How is he similar to the apostle Paul in 1 Corinthians 9? Write your reflections on how the fear of God relates to our treatment of those around us. (See Lev. 25:39–43.)

3. Pressing Through, with God's Help (6:1–19)

Nehemiah recounts a further series of threats (Neh. 6:1–14). Observe his process of responding. What can we learn from his various responses?

The final verses of chapter 6 (vv. 15–19) bring this section to a close—with what kind of resolution? What recurring themes are wound into these verses?

Read through the following sections on *Gospel Glimpses, Whole-Bible Connections*, and *Theological Soundings*. Then consider the *Personal Implications* these sections may have for you.

▶ Gospel Glimpses

PEOPLE BOUGHT OUT OF SLAVERY. Nehemiah objects to God's people enslaving one another due to unpaid debts. The most basic ground of his objection is not simply God's laws, but the history of God's deliverance that led to the giving of those laws. God's people have been delivered out of the slavery of exile, and they must not be enslaved again—nor must they enslave one another (Neh. 5:8). Deuteronomy 15:12–15 argues similarly: a fellow Hebrew who is enslaved to pay off a debt must be freed (and sent off with generous provision) after seven years, because the people must remember that they were slaves in Egypt, and God redeemed them. Nehemiah calls God's people to treat their brothers and sisters as those who have been redeemed. In the New Testament, this message grows into gospel fullness in light of God's redemption of us in Christ: "By this we know love, that he laid down his life for us, and we ought to lay down our lives for the brothers" (1 John 3:16).

SERVANTHOOD THAT CLAIMS NOTHING AND GIVES GENEROUSLY. We see in Nehemiah one who as governor could have "lorded it over the people" (Neh. 5:15) but who instead served them generously—gathering people from the nations at his table (vv. 17–18). Nehemiah did not claim the benefits of the allowance technically due him (vv. 14–18). We might think of the apostle Paul, who made no use of his God-given rights to payment for his gospel work (1 Cor. 9:14–15). For the sake of the Lord Jesus, he made himself "a servant to all" (1 Cor. 9:19). This kind of servanthood ultimately reflects a gospel-shaped pattern, shown most fully in Christ Jesus, who, "though he was in the form of God, did not count equality with God a thing to be grasped, but emptied himself, by taking the form of a servant" (Phil. 2:6–7). Through this heavenly servant, we receive by grace a salvation we do not deserve.

▶ Whole-Bible Connections

FEAR OF GOD. Nehemiah talks often about fear—of enemies (Neh. 4:14; 6:9, 14, 16, 19) and of God (1:11; 5:9, 15). He knows the "great and awesome" Lord (1:5), the only one worthy of fear—and the one who fights for his people and delivers them from fear of their enemies. Nehemiah understands David's words: "The LORD is my light and my salvation; whom shall I fear?" (Ps. 27:1). But he also understands Proverbs' words describing the fear of the Lord as the beginning of wisdom (Prov. 9:10). Nehemiah is a great example of Proverbs' wisdom, applying the fear of God to all of life and showing the kind of prudence and understanding celebrated in the Wisdom Literature. This includes the realm of social responsibility: addressing their injustice toward the needy, Nehemiah calls the people to "walk in the fear of our God" (Neh. 5:9). Jesus comes calling people to fear only the God in heaven, the one "who can destroy both soul and body in hell" (Matt. 10:28). He offers in himself the authoritative word on fear: "Do not fear, only believe" (Mark 5:36).

UNITY OF GOD'S PEOPLE. Chapter 3 offers a remarkable picture of God's people working together: the high priest, priests, Levites, and non–temple workers; goldsmiths and perfumers; servants and officers; people from towns near and far; father and daughters … one "next to" the other. It is a scene that reveals every single person's crucial role in God's family and that may anticipate the next stage in salvation history, when no longer would priest, prophet, or king be needed—other than Jesus Christ alone. In him, we believers are one, "fellow citizens with the saints and members of the household of God, … being built together into a dwelling place for God by the Spirit" (Eph. 2:19, 22).

▶ Theological Soundings

FAITH AND WORKS. How can Nehemiah in one breath cry, "Our God will fight for us," and in the next breath report, "So we labored at the work" (Neh. 4:20–21)? How shall we reconcile the two parts of this sentence: "We prayed to our God and set a guard as a protection against them day and night" (4:9)? The Bible calls for faith in God's sovereign work, and it urges work for which human beings are responsible. There is no need to reconcile the two; there is only need for human beings to trust and then, trusting, work! According to the apostle Paul, believers are saved by grace through faith, not as a result of works—but we are created in Christ Jesus for good works (Eph. 2:8–10).

Trusting in the God who fights for us, through Christ, each of us is empowered by Christ's very Spirit to "toil, struggling with all his energy that he powerfully works within [us]" (Col. 1:29).

LONGING FOR GOD'S JUSTICE. Through the thread of Nehemiah's sentence-prayers emerges a longing for God to make things right—to punish evil and reward good (Neh. 5:19; 6:14). Reading the Scriptures, we find Nehemiah's voice resonating with many of God's people who have longed for heavenly justice in the face of earthly injustice. "Mankind will say, 'Surely there is a reward for the righteous; surely there is a God who judges on earth'" (Ps. 58:11). Old Testament history ends not with perfect resolution but with intense longing. Malachi looks with longing toward a day bringing fiery judgment and the "sun of righteousness" rising "with healing in its wings" (Mal. 4:1–3). We who have welcomed the first coming of the Lord Jesus know that in him God's justice has been accomplished on behalf of sinners who trust him. And we long for the day of his second coming, when all evil will be punished, all will be made right, and all the longings of God's people will be met eternally in him.

> ## Personal Implications

Take time to reflect on the implications of Nehemiah 3–6 for your own life today. Consider what you have learned that might lead you to praise God, repent of sin, and trust in his gracious promises. Make notes below on the personal implications for your walk with the Lord of the (1) *Gospel Glimpses*, (2) *Whole-Bible Connections*, (3) *Theological Soundings*, and (4) this passage as a whole.

1. Gospel Glimpses

2. Whole-Bible Connections

3. Theological Soundings

_____

_____

_____

_____

_____

_____

4. Nehemiah 3–6

_____

_____

_____

_____

_____

_____

▶ As You Finish This Unit . . .

Take a moment now to ask for the Lord's blessing and help as you continue in this study. And take a moment also to look back through this unit of study, to reflect on some key things that the Lord may be teaching you—and perhaps to highlight and underline these things to review again in the future.

WEEK 9: PEOPLE REBUILDING—AROUND GOD'S WORD

Nehemiah 7–8

▲

The Place of the Passage

Now that the wall has been built (7:1), attention turns to building up the people. The physical heritage of these descendants of Abraham is clear as Nehemiah enrolls them by genealogy (ch. 7). Their spiritual heritage emerges as they are taught God's Word, handed down to them from the days of Moses (ch. 8).

The Big Picture

The focus now is on God's people: first is their enrollment according to a genealogy from Ezra's time (ch. 7), then their instruction in the Book of the Law (ch. 8).

> **Reflection and Discussion**

Read Nehemiah 7–8. Then write your reflections on the following questions. (For further background, see the *ESV Study Bible*, pages 835–838; available online at esv.org.)

1. Getting Organized (7:1–73)

How does Nehemiah 7:1–4 help us see Nehemiah's challenges and priorities in reestablishing the city of Jerusalem?

Take a moment to read Psalm 48 and remember how God's people regarded this city of Jerusalem. How does this psalm help show what Nehemiah (and ultimately what God) was seeking in restoring this city?

Read through the rest of chapter 7, mostly a reproduction of the list from Ezra 2. Why does Nehemiah consider it important to rehearse these genealogies and enroll the people of God in light of them?

2. Reading the Law (8:1–12)

Picture the scene in Nehemiah 8:1–6. What details stand out, particularly details showing attitudes toward the Word of God? Which attitudes do you find most challenging and convicting, especially as a member of Christ's body today?

The Levites moved among the people, helping them to understand what was being read. What words stand out in verses 7–8? What can we learn from this scene?

What might they have read in the Book of the Law of Moses that made them weep? Why do you think the priests and Levites urged them not to weep? What truths about joy can we learn in this scene?

3. The Word Keeps Working (8:13–18)

On the next day, who returns? What do they discover? Read the background in Leviticus 23:29–43 and comment on the people's response to this discovery.

Look back through Nehemiah 8 and list the ways you see God at work among his people through his Word. What several key words recur in this chapter? Looking at these summary notes, what do you find encouraging and convicting? How does this chapter lead you to pray?

Read through the following sections on *Gospel Glimpses*, *Whole-Bible Connections*, and *Theological Soundings*. Then consider the *Personal Implications* these sections may have for you.

Gospel Glimpses

PILGRIM PEOPLE. It must have been quite a sight—those little temporary huts in the squares and throughout the rundown city of Jerusalem. The Feast of Booths reminded the people of the hasty, divinely ordered exodus from Egypt and the journey through the wilderness. They now have been delivered again, this time from exile. And they are still on a journey through God's plan of salvation. The context of the ceremonial feast days (the Day of Atonement would also have been celebrated that month) highlights that the law they are reading is more than merely a set of rules—it is God's Word given to the people he delivered and made his own. Believers today are God's delivered people through the final deliverance accomplished by Christ at the cross— and indeed we are still pilgrims, walking in the light of God's Word toward the story's promised end.

GOSPEL REVEALED IN WORDS. After the exile, God's people become a nation focused on his written Word. The physical evidences of a kingdom are gone. Glorious Jerusalem is desolate. But they have God's Word to tell them who they are. As they repeatedly trace their seed, they are putting their faith in God's promises to Abraham. The process of taking in God's Word reveals their own story of a sinful people rescued by God. A faithful remnant continued to celebrate and preserve this Word through the following centuries until Jesus finally came and showed how the whole story was about him (John 5:39–47).

The New Testament writers completed the authoritative Word from God to reveal his gospel fully and finally in the Lord Jesus Christ. Now, until Christ comes again, we remain a people of God's written Word, understanding and living out the gospel as expressed in its inspired words.

Whole-Bible Connections

TEACHING GOD'S WORD. The big Bible study in chapter 8 represents not a newly discovered activity but the resumption of a biblical pattern—with increased intensity. The law itself commanded that it be taught diligently, generation by generation (Deut. 6:7). The wisdom literature was written to instruct people in the practice of godly wisdom. This Word is consistently presented as requiring learning, studying, processing—God himself being the ultimate Instructor, who by his Spirit applies the Word to our hearts. (See especially David's prayers concerning the Word—for example, Ps. 51:13; 119:33–34.) Jesus comes as the supreme Teacher, speaking with unique authority as he constantly expounds the Scriptures that reveal him. The present age is an age of teaching God's completed Scriptures to his growing church—with leaders in particular called to teach God's gathered people (1 Tim. 4:13), and all God's people called to teach his Word as they have learned it (Col. 3:16).

LIVING AND ACTIVE POWER OF GOD'S WORD. Reading this scene of God's people reading his Word, we glimpse remarkable layers of its power. As they began the books of Moses, they would have read how God spoke the world into being—and would have seen how through that word God was revealing himself, bringing conviction and transformation. The Word tells of prophets who brought God's word directly to his people. Finally came the Word-made-flesh, the Word through whom all things were made; it is he, the Lord Jesus, whom this written Word reveals from beginning to end (John 1:3; Luke 24:27). The power of these words to us today adds another layer of God's working, by his Spirit, in our hearts and minds as we read. To read in the Word about the Word at work is to receive live confirmation of its claims to be living and active, God-breathed, profitable in myriad ways, "sharper than any two-edged sword, piercing to the division of soul and of spirit" (2 Tim. 3:14–17; Heb. 4:12).

Theological Soundings

UNDERSTANDING OF GOD'S WORD. Understanding the Scriptures is more than an intellectual process. God, who breathed out these words by his Spirit, helps open minds and hearts as these words are read, taught, and received. As the word "understanding" weaves its way through Nehemiah 8 (vv. 2, 3, 7, 8, 12), we see not just transfer of information but teaching of God's divine revelation that brings people to weep, rejoice, worship, share— in other words, teaching that transforms, inside and out. When David prays for understanding, he implores a personal God: "Let my cry come before you, O Lord; give me understanding according to your word!" (Ps. 119:169). Paul writes to Timothy concerning suffering for the gospel, adding these encouraging words: "Think over what I say, for the Lord will give you understanding in everything" (2 Tim. 2:7). How encouraging, indeed, to hear the Word tell us that by God's grace we can understand it, with God's own help—not perfectly, but more and more.

JOY OF THE LORD. Joy is more than a desirable emotion. The joy of the Lord in Nehemiah 8:9–12 is repeatedly connected to the holiness of this feast day gathering: "This day is holy," say the leaders three times. So do not weep— but be joyful. The joy of the Lord flows from the very character of the Lord, particularly his holiness that sets him apart from any created thing. And his people (amazingly, miraculously) get to come near that holiness and actually participate in it—*that* is joy. Being near him, we become like him: The joy of the Lord is your strength. This joy happens only as we are cleansed, forgiven of our sin; otherwise, we could not draw near. Isaiah makes clear the source of joy: "With joy you will draw water from the wells of salvation" (12:3). The apostle Paul commands this same joy for believers, joy in the person of the God who saves us through his Son: "Rejoice in the Lord [Jesus] always" (Phil. 4:4).

Personal Implications

Take time to reflect on the implications of Nehemiah 7–8 for your own life today. Consider what you have learned that might lead you to praise God, repent of sin, and trust in his gracious promises. Make notes below on the personal implications for your walk with the Lord of the (1) *Gospel Glimpses*, (2) *Whole-Bible Connections*, (3) *Theological Soundings*, and (4) this passage as a whole.

1. Gospel Glimpses

2. Whole-Bible Connections

3. Theological Soundings

4. Nehemiah 7–8

Take a moment now to ask for the Lord's blessing and help as you continue in this study. And take a moment also to look back through this unit, to reflect on some key things that the Lord may be teaching you—and perhaps to highlight and underline these things to review again in the future.

WEEK 10: CONFESSION— IN RESPONSE TO GOD'S WORD

Nehemiah 9–10

▲

The Place of the Passage

In chapter 8, the leaders told the people not to weep but to rejoice. But there is a time for weeping—and that time has now come. The confession[1] and repentance[2] in chapters 9–10 build directly upon the reading and teaching of the law in the previous chapters. This has been a Word-filled month. Revival is happening, and it happens as God works in his people, by his Spirit and through his Word. The first half of Nehemiah showed the rebuilding of walls; as the second half develops, we are watching the rebuilding of a people—from the inside out.

The Big Picture

Convicted by their reading and study of the law, the people confess their sin in light of the history revealed in that law (ch. 9), and they renew their covenant promises to obey that law (ch. 10).

Reflection and Discussion

Read Nehemiah 9–10. Then write your reflections on the following questions. (For further background, see the *ESV Study Bible*, pages 838–841; available online at esv.org.)

1. Prayer of Confession (9:1–38)

List all the carefully noted elements of this prayer gathering (Neh. 9:1–5). What strikes you in Nehemiah's description of God's people coming together in prayer—and what can we learn from this scene today?

Chapter 9 records the longest prayer in the Bible, giving a sweeping review of Israel's history. Read verses 6–31 and construct a general outline of the sections. Why do you think this prayer is so full of history—and why is this important?

How does each sentence in verses 6–15 begin? What various attributes of God are celebrated in these verses? (Consider: Do we tell our history in this way? If not, should we? Why or why not?)

Verse 16 brings a significant occurrence of "But," leading to what important revelations about the Israelites (and all of us)? Verse 17b brings another "But," leading to what important revelations about the character of God and his ways with his people (vv. 17b–25)?

Create your own chart of the logical twists and turns in verses 26–31. How would you sum up the pattern here? What key words do you find, and how are they significant?

Verse 32 finally arrives at "now." In what several ways does the final section of this prayer (vv. 32–37) effectively sum up what has come before? What and how are the people asking God?

For those of us who have the completed Scriptures and who know Jesus Christ by name, how will our prayers be both similar to and different from the prayer in Nehemiah 9? (Consider, for example, the perspective of Hebrews 13:10–21.)

2. Covenant Promises (10:1–39)

The people's "firm covenant" comes about "because of all this" (Neh. 9:38). To what does "all this" refer? For further clarification, read on in Nehemiah 10:1–29. What has impressed and motivated these people, and how can we tell?

In what specific areas of the law do the people focus their promises (10:30–39)? In the context of what you've seen so far in Ezra and Nehemiah, why are these areas so crucial for the people to focus on?

In light of Ezra's ending and the history revealed in the prayer of chapter 9 of Nehemiah, what questions might we have about the people's covenant in chapter 10? Read again Nehemiah 9:17. Read also Exodus 34:1–9. What glorious truths about God stand out?

Read through the following sections on *Gospel Glimpses*, *Whole-Bible Connections*, and *Theological Soundings*. Then take time to consider the *Personal Implications* these sections may have for you.

Gospel Glimpses

GOD'S MERCIES.[3] The mercies of God run like a stream through Nehemiah chapter 9, answering the disobedience of the people repeatedly with something much better than they deserved. The first mention of mercy (v. 17) directly echoes Exodus 34:5–6, in which God proclaimed his name before Moses and then rewrote the two tablets of the law—after Moses had broken the first ones in anger over the people's sin. Verses 18–19 of Nehemiah 9 recall the making of a golden calf and God's "great mercies" in not forsaking this blasphemous people. The language of "saviors" and "deliverers" (vv. 27–28) points clearly ahead to the Savior who came to deliver his people finally from sin. The prayer's sweep of history climaxes in a statement bookended by mercy: "In your great mercies you did not make an end of them or forsake them, for you are a gracious and merciful God" (v. 31).

STIFFENED NECKS. Scripture has many ways to talk of sin's deserving of wrath. One vivid picture throughout the Old Testament is that of stiffening one's neck—refusing, like a stubborn mule, to take direction (9:17, 29). The people rebel against God by constructing a golden calf and then in effect become like what they worship: God immediately nicknames them "stiff-necked" (Ex. 32:9). They are bovine, stubborn, disobedient, and running wild (see Neh. 9:16, 17, 26, 29). After the prayer's exaltation of the God who alone is Lord and the rehearsing of his mercies to his people, this picture makes rebellion against him appear even more willful—and foolish. It also confirms the fact that salvation comes to us disobedient rebels with absolutely no help or deserving on our part; salvation of those with stiffened necks is accomplished wholly by the Lord, due wholly to his mercy (Eph. 2:1–9).

Whole-Bible Connections

THE BIBLE'S STORY OF GOD'S COVENANTS. As the prayer in chapter 9 sweeps through salvation history, it tells a story of God's covenants with his people. In connection with Abraham, the part of the covenant involving the land is emphasized, as these exiles who have been returned to their land celebrate God's keeping his promise (Neh. 9:8; see Ps. 105:8–11). The story uses covenant language throughout; for example, God "multiplied their children as the stars of heaven" (Neh. 9:23; Gen. 15:5). Their appeal for mercy is to the "great, the mighty, and the awesome God, who keeps covenant and steadfast love" (Neh. 9:32). These people are calling out to God to continue to be faithful to his promises, even though they have been unfaithful (9:33). Not only did God faithfully protect this remnant through the next centuries, but from them he brought the Lord Jesus in the line of David, just as he had covenanted to do.

Jesus came as the fulfillment of all God's promises (2 Cor. 1:20) and the inaugurator of a new covenant, one ratified by his blood (Matt. 26:28; 1 Cor. 11:25).

GOD'S ABUNDANT PROVISION. God gave Adam and Eve a garden of abundant food—all but one tree (Gen. 1:29; 2:16–17). After they sinned by eating of the forbidden tree, and forfeited that abundance, the rest of the story tells of God making a way to provide for his sinful people, abundantly. The Promised Land is "flowing with milk and honey" (Ex. 3:17; 33:3; Deut. 31:20). Nehemiah 9:25 echoes Moses' description of the land's riches (Deut. 6:10–12). Moses warned that the people would become full and forget the Lord—and so they did, and the abundance was taken away. Yet here in Nehemiah we see God's abundant mercies flowing. That mercy culminates in the One whose giving was reflected in all those physical riches: Jesus Christ. He came so that his followers might have life, and have it abundantly (John 10:10). In him we inherit all the riches of the new heaven and earth—trees of Eden-like abundance and God dwelling fully in our very midst, with the slain and risen Lamb of God as the temple and the lamp, lighting the whole scene with his glory (Rev. 21:22–23; 22:1–5).

> ## Theological Soundings

LAW AS BLESSING. After this month of assemblies, the people have rediscovered the joy of hearing and obeying God's Word. Every mention of it in chapter 9 reflects the good source and great blessing of hearing the "book of the Law of the LORD their God" (9:3). Among the mercies enumerated in the prayer is the awesome fact that God "came down on Mount Sinai and spoke with them from heaven and gave them right rules and true laws, good statutes and commandments" (9:13). These people are celebrating what we sometimes struggle to understand—the uses of the Old Testament law. John Calvin and other church fathers celebrated the law as useful, first as a mirror to reflect God's righteousness and our sin. This scene of confession vividly shows that use, as well as its use in restraining evil: the prayer is followed directly by a renewed covenant to obey. Finally, we see here the use of the law in glorifying God by revealing what is pleasing to him and the beauty of his own character. These are indeed "good statutes" (9:13; see also Ps. 19:7–11).

THE RIGHTEOUSNESS[4] OF GOD. The law with its "right rules" reveals the character of God—not only his mercies but also his righteousness. Why has he kept his covenant with this sinful people? Is he merely sorry for them? No: "You have kept your promise, for you are righteous" (9:8). God's faithfulness to his word is God's faithfulness to his own righteous self. The prayer asks for more mercy, but it never complains that the suffering of God's people is unjust: "You have been righteous in all that has come upon us, for you have dealt faithfully and we have acted wickedly" (9:33). These affirmations of God's righteousness make God's mercies shine out even more brightly. They also push our gaze forward to see how God's righteousness will finally be satisfied. The apostle Paul explains: God put forward his perfectly righteous Son "as a propitiation by his blood, to be received by faith. This was to show God's righteousness, because in his divine forbearance he had passed over former sins. It was to show his righteousness at the present time, so that he might be both just and the justifier of the one who has faith in Jesus" (see Rom. 3:25–26).

Personal Implications

Reflect on the implications of Nehemiah 9–10 for your own life today. Consider what you have learned that might lead you to praise God, repent of sin, and trust in his gracious promises. Make notes below on the personal implications for your walk with the Lord of the (1) *Gospel Glimpses*, (2) *Whole-Bible Connections*, (3) *Theological Soundings*, and (4) this passage as a whole.

1. Gospel Glimpses

2. Whole-Bible Connections

3. Theological Soundings

4. Nehemiah 9–10

▶ **As You Finish This Unit . . .**

Take a moment now to ask for the Lord's blessing and help as you continue in this study. Take a moment also to look back through this unit, to reflect on some key things that the Lord may be teaching you—and perhaps to highlight and underline these things to review again in the future.

Definitions

[1] **Confession** – Public acknowledgment of belief (2 Cor. 9:13; Heb. 4:14) or of sin (Ezra 10:1; James 5:16; 1 John 1:9).

[2] **Repentance** – A complete change of heart and mind regarding one's overall attitude toward God or one's individual actions. True regeneration and conversion are always accompanied by repentance.

[3] **Mercy** – Compassion and kindness toward someone experiencing hardship, sometimes even when such suffering results from the person's own sin or foolishness. God displays mercy toward his people and they, in turn, are called to display mercy toward others (Luke 6:36).

[4] **Righteousness** – The quality of being morally right and without sin. One of God's distinctive attributes. God imputes righteousness to (justifies) those who trust in Jesus Christ.

WEEK 11: CELEBRATION—
IN LIGHT OF
GOD'S WORD

Nehemiah 11–12

▲

The Place of the Passage

Chapters 11–12 show the ongoing fruit of the revival seen in the previous chapters. The dedication of the wall is the highlight of this section, coming, appropriately, not immediately after the physical rebuilding but after the spiritual rebuilding that has occurred.

The Big Picture

This section shows God's people together living out the faith they've affirmed: repopulating Jerusalem, celebrating in corporate worship, and institutionalizing ongoing temple worship.

Reflection and Discussion

Read Nehemiah 11–12. Then write your reflections on the following questions. (For further background, see the *ESV Study Bible*, pages 841–845; available online at esv.org.)

1. Filling Jerusalem with God's People (11:1–12:26)

Recall the significance of this city for the people of God. From what you have seen in Ezra and Nehemiah so far, how would you explain the fact that Jerusalem is called the "holy city" (11:1, 18)?

Recall the description of this city in Nehemiah 7:1–4. Obviously, people had been taking the more comfortable choice of resettling in surrounding towns. How does the process of repopulating Jerusalem show God's gracious working among his people (11:1–2)?

Read Nehemiah 11:3–12:26. What details and emphases do you notice? Read 1 Chronicles 9:17–34 for background.

2. Dedicating the Wall (12:27–43)

Read of the preparations for this ceremony (12:27–30). What aspects stand out? Read the background of purification ceremonies in Exodus 19:10–15. Although we do not conduct such ceremonies today, what might we learn from this preparation for worship?

Notice in 12:31 that Nehemiah has returned as the masterful administrator. (His first-person voice left temporarily after 7:5.) As you read verses 31–43, try to see, hear, and feel what this great gathering must have witnessed. Draw a simple picture that helps you imagine it. Ponder what this scene must have meant to those gathered, many of whom had helped rebuild the wall they were now walking on. Write your thoughts and comments.

What words in verses 27–43 show the attitudes of people's hearts? Where have you found these words before in Ezra and Nehemiah? How would you sum up what these books are teaching us about the attitudes of our hearts in worship?

Notice the final phrase in Nehemiah 12:43 and in Ezra 3:13. How do you think the surrounding peoples responded to this sound? In what ways is joy a crucial witness to the world around God's people?

3. Institutionalizing Temple Service (12:44–47)

Nehemiah 12:44–47 brings us back to everyday life, with nitty-gritty details necessary to institutionalize corporate commitments. Sum up the focus of the organization in these verses. What are the people aiming for here? What guides do they follow in getting organized?

The joy does not disappear! What is the focus of the joy in these verses? What can we learn here? In what ways might this passage and this lesson's chapters (chs. 11–12) encourage us today as we think about ordering our lives as God's joyful people in this needy world?

Read through the following sections on *Gospel Glimpses*, *Whole-Bible Connections*, and *Theological Soundings*. Then take time to consider the *Personal Implications* these sections may have for you.

Gospel Glimpses

JOYFUL SACRIFICES FROM A REDEEMED PEOPLE. These chapters show God's people offering joyful sacrifices to God their Redeemer. He has rescued them from exile and brought them home to Jerusalem, where they are now able to live and worship safely within its walls. All this is by God's hand, and they are responding to his provision. They offer songs of thanksgiving and "great sacrifices"—on this day, and then in the days that follow with regular songs of worship, offerings, and "daily portions" (Neh. 12:43, 47). The contours of this story are the contours of God's redeemed people in all times. As Jesus Christ our Redeemer has come and rescued us from the slavery of sin, giving us eternally secure life in him, we as God's people "continually offer up a sacrifice of praise to God" with the praises of our lips and with the whole of our lives (Heb. 13:15; Rom. 12:1).

PRIESTS AND LEVITES. These books have overflowed with names of priests, Levites, and temple workers, all filling important leadership roles prescribed by God in his law. Through priests, in particular, God showed a sinful people's need to be represented before a holy God; through the elaborate ceremonial system, God showed how much help we need in order to approach him. If we enter his presence without help, we will die. The wonder, then, is that God sent his own Son to help us fully and finally. All the long lists of priests in the world could not do so. These priests merely prepare us for Jesus Christ, the Son of God, who alone fulfilled the role of high priest. He offered himself as the final perfect sacrifice so that no more priests are needed—as every cleansed believer joins the chosen race and royal priesthood (Heb. 10:19–22; 1 Pet. 2:9).

Whole-Bible Connections

JERUSALEM'S STRONG WALLS. These walls must have been strong enough to support these processions of great choirs, despite Tobiah's taunting that even a fox could break down the Israelites' stone wall (Neh. 4:3). This celebration of rebuilt walls is a celebration of God's provision of safety for his people, protecting them against all their enemies. In Scripture this city of Jerusalem becomes a growing picture of the wonderful security of God's redeemed people. The prophet Isaiah peers into the distance and envisions a "strong city," where God "sets up salvation as walls and bulwarks" and the gates are opened for the righteous to enter (Isa. 26:1–3). Isaiah speaks of walls called "Salvation" and gates called "Praise" (Isa. 60:18). The "holy city, new Jerusalem" of Revelation 21 also has a "great, high wall, with twelve gates" that "will never be shut by day—and there will be no night there" (Rev. 21:2, 10–14, 25–26). The walls of the heavenly Jerusalem are the walls of salvation accomplished in Christ, secure for eternity.

SONGS OF PRAISE. The dedication of the wall resounds with singing to the Lord, with repeated mention of two great "choirs that gave thanks" (Neh. 12:31)—a phrase translating one Hebrew word meaning "thanksgivings." What did they sing? They used instruments "of David the man of God" (v. 36), so it would not be surprising if they were singing words of David as well—perhaps psalms of thanksgiving to the Lord. Many of David's psalms call for God's people to "Come into his presence with singing!"—"I will sing of steadfast love and justice; to you, O LORD, I will make music" (Ps. 100:2; 101:1). Jesus sang hymns (psalms) with his followers (Matt. 26:30), and the Epistles assume those in the church will do the same (Col. 3:16). All this singing of God's people echoes the singing in the heavenly places right now to God and to the Lamb (Rev. 4:8–11; 5:9–14). The prospect of eternity in God's presence is one of joining in a universe-wide song of praise.

> ## Theological Soundings

PURIFICATION FROM SIN. Nehemiah 12:30 suggests the comprehensive requirements of the purification rituals: the priests and Levites purified themselves, people, gates, wall . . . basically everything! The law vividly illustrates the infiltration of sin's impurity into every nook and cranny of existence. Since the fall, all creation has been in "bondage to corruption" (Rom. 8:20–22). Gloriously, Jesus' death and resurrection conquered sin and death; believers are no longer in bondage and can draw near to God "with a true heart in full assurance of faith, with our hearts sprinkled clean from an evil conscience and our bodies washed with pure water" (Heb. 10:22). Praise God! We require no purification rituals to come into his presence; we come claiming the blood of Jesus, who himself made purification for sins (Heb. 1:3). However, until Jesus comes again and our sanctification is complete, we do battle with sin in a world groaning in its bondage to corruption. The hope for those in Christ is this: "If we confess our sins, he is faithful and just to forgive us our sins and to cleanse us from all unrighteousness" (1 John 1:9).

LOOKING FOR A KING IN THE LINE OF DAVID. Chapter 12 abounds with references to David—mostly in relation to worship and music (Neh. 12:24, 36, 37, 45, 46). As we approach the end of this book and of recorded Old Testament history, national prospects for God's people look bleak. God grants the blessing of being restored as a people to worship in his temple—indeed, part of the point is that they must now grasp these spiritual blessings, having lost the physical blessings of their own kingdom with their own king. But what about this king? What is *not* mentioned in relation to David is perhaps as important as what *is* mentioned: everyone knew God had promised a great king to come in David's line. The covenant with David was recorded and passed down, even in the psalms these people sang and compiled at this time (Ps. 89:34–37; 132:11). Had the people lost hope in this promise? As they clung to the heritage of "David the man of God" (Neh. 12:24, 36), surely the air was heavy with the promise that an eternal king would sit on his throne. Old Testament history ends with this promise hanging in the air—to be fulfilled only with the coming of the King himself, announcing that the "kingdom of God is at hand" (Mark 1:15).

Personal Implications

Take time to reflect on the implications of Nehemiah 11–12 for your own life today. Consider what you have learned that might lead you to praise God, repent of sin, and trust in his gracious promises. Make notes below on the personal implications for your walk with the Lord of the (1) *Gospel Glimpses*, (2) *Whole-Bible Connections*, (3) *Theological Soundings*, and (4) this passage as a whole.

1. Gospel Glimpses

2. Whole-Bible Connections

3. Theological Soundings

4. Nehemiah 11–12

As You Finish This Unit . . .

Take a moment now to ask for the Lord's blessing and help as you move into the final chapter of Nehemiah. Take a moment also to look back through this unit, to reflect on some key things that the Lord may be teaching you—and perhaps to highlight and underline these things to review again in the future.

Week 12: Summary and Conclusion

(Including Nehemiah 13)

▲

We will conclude our study of Ezra and Nehemiah by summarizing the big picture of God's message through these two narratives. Included in that summary will be consideration of Nehemiah's concluding chapter, which provides an enlightening end piece to this part of salvation history. We will then consider several questions in order to reflect on various Gospel Glimpses, Whole-Bible Connections, and Theological Soundings.

The Big Picture of Ezra and Nehemiah

Ezra and Nehemiah together show God's faithfulness to his promises: he has promised to bless Abraham's seed, and here they are, preserved as a people, delivered from the Babylonian exile, restored to the land of promise and the holy city, and worshiping at the rebuilt temple according to God's law. All this is due only to God's steadfast love and his hand of favor on his people (see Ezra 9:8–9).

All this makes these postexilic books sound like a really happy ending to Old Testament history, but they are not. We've read them through—but now stop and take a moment to reread carefully the final chapter of Nehemiah, asking yourself as you read, Why does the story end here?

What a final chapter! We might wish that Nehemiah had concluded with the joyful celebration of chapter 12. It is significant that neither Ezra nor Nehemiah allows us to settle down into resolution at the end of their narratives; these are matching non-resolutions to one part of a larger story that has not yet reached its climax. That is the point. The climax is yet to come—400 years later. Nehemiah ends this whole postexilic drama by showing a needy people and a needy leader peering forward in the dark, looking for the light to come.

This story ends in the dark because it is not fully over. First and foremost, the story is not over because the promised seed has not yet appeared. This part of the story shows the blessing of the ceremonial temple worship God instituted so that his people could approach him in worship and live in communion with him. But all those priests and sacrifices were pointing forward to the one priest, the one sacrifice: the Lord Jesus. He is the promised seed to come from this people. He is the Light of the World, and the pathway to him through history is full of shadows until the light shines.

The shadows are shadows of sin: sin in the enemies all around, who are rebelling against the one true God by trying to destroy his people, their holy city, and their distinct worship; and sin in God's people themselves. Both Ezra and Nehemiah close with a reemergence of serious sin among the people after promises to obey and reform. All of it is sin that would destroy the "holy race" of Abraham from which the promised seed will come. Intermarriage in particular threatens the purity of God's people—those who are called to serve him alone and from whom will come the promised seed (Gen. 12:7).

What we understand in all these shadows is the need for the seed. These people and this world cannot save themselves. They are not good enough. Even God's called-out people, blessed with his favor, cannot be good enough. Great leaders like Ezra and Nehemiah cannot make it happen—in the end they are either pulling out their hair, pulling out others' hair, or crying out in the dark to God for help.

But therein lies the hope: it is in God, and only in God. This weak, struggling remnant is in God's hand; we see that truth clearly right from the start of each book. The people cannot keep their covenants, but we are reading the Word of "the great, the mighty, and the awesome God, who keeps covenant and steadfast love" (Neh. 9:32; see also 1:5). We see his people commune with him in prayer, and we see his Word at work among them. They are his people. He gives them joy as they worship and obey him. There is no doubt in these books that, in spite of all the shadows, and even through the weakness of his people, God is working his plan of salvation that will not only bless this people and their seed, but will through that seed bless all the nations of the world.

Gospel Glimpses

Where is the gospel in these Old Testament narratives? They certainly do not teach about Jesus' death and resurrection. Rather, they show the truth of the gospel as lived out by the imperfect people through whom God worked his redemptive plan, with Jesus at the center of it. This part of the story is especially poignant because we see God's merciful hand delivering his people after the punishment and scattering of the exile; we see both the nature of sinful people who need deliverance, and the mercy of a God who delivers such a people. But this story, as we've seen, perches on the dark edge of Old Testament history and leans forward almost agonizingly to the opening of the New Testament, when the promised seed, the promised Deliverer, comes to save his people fully and finally.

Have Ezra and Nehemiah brought new clarity to your understanding of the gospel? How so?

Which particular passages or themes in Ezra and Nehemiah helped you see the scope and beauty of God's redemptive plan, and perhaps led you to a fresh understanding of God's grace to us through Jesus?

Whole-Bible Connections

These postexilic narratives offer a crucial connecting link in the redemptive story, bringing the promised remnant of God's people back together in Jerusalem, set in place for the long intertestamental wait culminating in Jesus' coming. It is a period in biblical history with which many can identify as we see God's merciful hand on this weak, struggling remnant. It is helpful to connect these books with the prophets who brought God's Word during this period: Haggai, Zechariah, and Malachi. Just as those prophets light up this history, so this history lights up those prophetic books—all together showing a God who is faithful to his promises and who calls his people to follow him faithfully according to his Word.

How has this study of Ezra and Nehemiah filled out your understanding of the biblical storyline of redemption?

Which themes emphasized in Ezra and Nehemiah have helped you deepen your grasp of the Bible's unity?

What connections between Old and New Testaments were new to you?

Theological Soundings

Ezra and Nehemiah have much to contribute to Christian theology, not through direct teaching but through narrative that tells the truth about God's nature and his redemptive plan. Numerous doctrines and themes are developed, clarified, and reinforced throughout these books, such as the sovereignty and mercy of God, the sinfulness of humanity, the need for a perfect deliverer,

God's unfailing covenant promises, and the sure redemption in Christ toward which the Old Testament ceremonial system points.

Has your theology shifted in minor or major ways during the course of studying Ezra and Nehemiah? If so, how?

How has your understanding of the nature and character of God been deepened throughout this study?

What unique contributions do Ezra and Nehemiah make toward our understanding of who Jesus is and what he accomplished through his life, death, and resurrection?

What, specifically, do these books teach us about the human condition and our need of redemption?

Personal Implications

God inspired the books of Ezra and Nehemiah in order to reveal himself to us and thereby transform us. As you reflect on these books, and as you look through your answers to the questions above, what implications do you see for your life?

What have you learned in these books that might lead you to praise God, turn away from sin, or trust more firmly in his promises?

As You Finish Studying Ezra and Nehemiah . . .

We rejoice with you as you finish studying these books! May this study become part of your Christian walk of faith, day by day and week by week throughout all your life. Now we would greatly encourage you to study the Word of God on a week-by-week basis. To continue your study of the Bible, we would encourage you to consider other books in the *Knowing the Bible* series, and to visit knowingthebibleseries.org.

Lastly, take a moment to look back through this study. Review the notes that you have written, and the things that you have highlighted or underlined. Reflect again on the key themes that the Lord has been teaching you about himself and about his Word. May these things become a treasure for you throughout your life—this we pray in the name of the Father, and the Son, and the Holy Spirit. Amen.